16-1-94

Greg,

Happy ...

with lots of love

Catherine, Jon,

Oliver, Arthur and

Harriet
XX.

Bin Ends

Bin Ends

Alan Coren

 Robson Books

The author would like to thank the proprietors of *Punch* magazine for permission to reproduce material in this book.

First published in Great Britain in 1987 by Robson Books Ltd., Bolsover House, 5–6 Clipstone Street, London W1P 7EB.

British Library Cataloguing in Publication Data

Bin Ends
Coren, Alan
    Bin Ends
    I. Title
    828'.91407   PN6175

ISBN 0-86051-465-X

Typesetting by concept, Crayford, Kent

Printed and bound in Great Britain by Adlard & Son Ltd., The Garden City Press, Letchworth, Herts.

For Fi and Roger

Contents

Etymologicon

Around ten years ago, in what posterity may well conclude was a somewhat fallow period for English literature, the publishing industry directed its cultural commitment towards the gumming of lists.

There was many a Book Of Lists, and they sold with depressing vigour. Their creative pattern never varied: a publisher would haul a couple of unemployed graduates from the parapet of Waterloo Bridge and offer them a blanket and a pittance, in return for which they would telephone two hundred semi-household names and beg them for a list of something – silliest vegetables, worthiest noises, favourite vermin, and so on – and the researchers would note all these down and hobble round to the publisher with them.

The publisher would then lunch a celebrity and wheedle him into bolting his name to the front of the book for little more than the combined lifetime incomes of the two graduates. The book could then become *Charlie Celebrity's Big Book of Lists* and sell in millions to punters who had heard him talking about it on *The Charlie Celebrity Show*.

Eventually, a very small publisher who knew a very small celebrity got around to a very small semi-household name and a very small graduate rang me. They were, whispered the indented wretch, compiling a list of favourite words, with the working title *Charlie Small's Big Book of Favourite Words*. Several hundred people were being asked for ten words each.

I gave them my ten favourite words, *peristaltic, vole, hone, widdle*, that sort of thing, ending with the most favoured of all.

It came out as *bim*.

Clearly, the very small publisher also had a very small proofreader.

The whole purpose of this preface – and indeed the title it

supports – is thus to make amends. While *bim* is unquestionably a delightful word, it cannot begin to approach the stunning richness of *bin*, not least because it doesn't mean anything.

Whereas *bin*, despite its one fleeting syllable, means virtually everything. It contains bread (for life) and wine (for joy) and both (for salvation).

As a salutary memento mori, however, it also contains dust.

And waste.

And, of course, loony.

Just how far each of these hyphenated options relates to what now follows is not for me to say.

A. C., 1987

Household Gods

Archaeologists are getting their first insight into the philosophy of one of Britain's earliest organized religions. They have unearthed evidence of the religious beliefs held by people 5,000 years ago at what appears to have been a Stone Age ritual centre near Peterborough.

One burial complex consisted of a cremated body, a severed dog's head, an upside down pot resembling a human cranium, a deliberately smashed red deer antler, shattered axe-heads and cattle bones. At the centre was a large corn-grinding stone deliberately positioned on its edge with a pestle under it, rather than on top, the normal position.

It may, however, be some time before the exact nature of the religion is fully understood.

the Independent

'YOU'LL LIKE this,' he said. He held it up.

She paused in her grinding, and wiped her hands on the goat.

'What is it?' she said.

'It's a gate,' he replied.

A child, possibly male, scuttled up on all fours and began licking flour off the goat. Its mother, deceptively agile for one so spheroid, clubbed the child smartly, and picked its hair off the pestle. The child bawled formally for a moment or two, then waddled back across the cave, dipped a forefinger in its new wound, and, tongue curled over its prognathous upper lip, began drawing on the wall.

'OY!' cried its father. His hurled axe-head shattered beside the infant.

'Stop that,' snapped his wife. 'Education is my responsibility.'

'He's put a winkle on the buffalo,' protested her husband. 'I did not spend a week decorating that wall in

11

order to have it outrage public decency. I trust you have not forgotten that the new people next door are coming in tonight for a full dough dinner with all the trimmings? They are a very respectable couple. She's had both her things painted to simulate rocks. Connected by a little chain going round her neck. Very chic.'

'Money down the drain,' said his wife. 'Anyone can tell they're not rocks. She only has to sneeze.'

'That is neither here nor there,' said her husband. 'I do not want her sitting through dinner staring at a bison's credentials. It's bright red, blood. Look at it. Your eye goes straight to it. They'll think we're common as muck. I might as well put this gate straight back in the cow for all the good it'll do.'

He held up the rough oblong of thong-bound ribs and shook it. A clavicle fell off.

'What's it for?' asked his wife.

'It's for the end of the path,' replied her husband.

Her thin brow furrowed. At the shock, something jumped out of her fringe, hopped about a bit, and vanished into the goat.

'You what?' she said.

Her husband rolled his little eyes.

'A path,' he said, 'is a flat item that sort of pokes out in front of a home. When you have smart people in for dinner, they have to walk up it. In order to walk up it, they have to push open a gate.'

'I do not see,' said his wife, 'why they can't just come round the corner of the hole.'

'Without knocking?' cried her husband. 'It would be unthinkable!'

His wife pondered this for a time. Finally, she said: 'Yes, it is.'

Her husband put the gate down, and went out, and came back in with another skeletal assembly. It was considerably more femoral than the first.

'That's a big gate,' said his wife. 'There's enough soup in that for a month.'

'It is not a gate,' said her husband, 'it is a door. It is what visitors knock on. Like this.'

He placed the door in the entrance hole and banged it with his knuckles. It fell to its constituent bits.

'Is it supposed to do that?' she enquired.

Her husband, having hitherto only heard about knocking and not actually tried it, said:

'Yes.'

'There's a lot of work goes into these dinner parties,' said his wife.

'You don't get owt for nowt in this life,' said her husband.

'I beg your pardon?'

'Small talk,' he explained, somewhat smugly. 'You hear it in all the best places. For example, who's she the cat's mother. There's more to this than meets the eye, that's another good one. You just pop 'em in when it goes quiet. By the way, it needs a rat on it.'

'I like that one,' she said. 'By the way, it needs a rat on it. I'll remember that.'

'No, no, no!' he shouted, with such reverberant force that everything that had recently hopped into the goat now hopped on to the child. 'That was not one of them! I was talking about the door. The *door* will need a rat on it.'

His wife looked at him for a while, then returned to the grinding.

'Yes,' he said, 'I thought that would impress you. I thought you would have no reply to that. There is no need to thank me. It is my job, ensuring that we go up in the world. You may now inform your friends and relatives that we live at Number Rat.'

'Number Rat, eh?' said his wife, carefully.

'As soon, that is, as I have put the door together again and hung a suitable rat on it, thereby distinguishing ourselves from our new neighbours at Number Hedgehog.'

'Aha!' cried his wife, stopping in mid-pestle. 'There's more to this than meets the eye!'

'Very good,' he said. 'You see what you can do if you really try? Nobody would guess your father ate people.'

'They've got a gate and a path and a door at the end with a hedgehog on it, then?'

'Put it all up this morning,' he said, nodding. 'Not to put too fine a point on it – that's another good one, incidentally, ideal for most occasions – this has now become a neighbourhood. It has always been a dream of mine to live at Number Rat, the Neighbourhood. Stone me,' he cried, ignoring the attendant risk, 'do you realize that if we could only persuade that bastard on the other side to kick his gibbon out and find a more suitable consort, we could very well become a Residential Suburb!'

'He could make a door and hang her on it,' said his wife, somewhat heavily. 'It could be Number Gibbon.'

Her husband looked up.

'Is anything wrong?' he enquired.

'Only that it is a mistake to run,' replied his wife, 'before you can, er, – what's that thing where your knuckles come off the ground and you fall over?'

'Lager?' said her husband. 'The stuff that bubbled out of the nuts last year? I do not quite –'

A shadow touched his small toe, and he jumped.

'Crikey, that's never the time, is it?' he cried. 'They'll be here any something!'

In the event, all was ready. The sun was low, and the door fell off.

'Oh, dear!' said the woman from Number Hedgehog.

'Ho, yes, absolutely!' cried her host, ushering her inside. 'Oh dear, indeed! Who's she the cat's mother? You don't get owt for nowt in this life.'

The woman from Number Hedgehog glanced at her husband, who was attached to a long thin thong that disappeared beyond the now doorless hole.

'Your door –' began the woman again.

'Yes, a little winner, isn't it?' cried the man from Number Rat. 'You only have to look at it and it's off. By the way, may I enquire what that is on your husband's wrist? Something fashionable, I'll be bound!'

'It's our dog,' said the man from Number Hedgehog. He tugged on the thong, and a wall-eyed yellow animal lurched into the cave and sank its fangs greedily into the pile of door.

'Put it down, Spot!' cried its master, but the dog merely scuttled into the far darkness and began crunching invisibly.

'I'm sorry,' said the man, 'but I'm afraid he is not yet fully domesticated.'

'Think nothing of it,' replied the host. 'It is only a hinge he has got hold of. We have an entire cowful out back. On the patio.'

'Ah,' said his neighbour.

'Imagine taming a dog!' exclaimed the man from Number Rat. 'It means you can take it about without it going for you! It means you are never without a fresh meal. Dearest,' he called into the murky recess, 'the people next door have brought a dog!'

His wife emerged from the smoke.

'What am I going to do with all this dough, then?' she said.

'Ha, ha, they are taming it to eat *later*!' explained her husband.

'What we did bring you,' said the woman from Number Hedgehog, quickly, 'is this rather interesting pot.' She took it out, and looked around. 'Do you have an occasional table?'

'An occasional table, an occasional table!' cried the man from Number Rat. 'Goodness me, you don't get a cat's mother for owt, now where did I put that occasional table, well I never did, there's more in this than meets . . .'

He disappeared into the rear of the cave. The other three stared at one another. Throats were cleared. The dog howled, once. And then, on a rumbling sound, the householder reappeared. He was dragging the grinding-stone, and had the pestle in his teeth.

'Leg came off,' he gasped.

He heaved the stone on to its edge, and jammed it steady with the pestle.

'Very nice,' said the woman from Number Hedgehog. 'Rough-hewn, perhaps, but, as a decor statement, frank. It says what it is.'

'It says it's a grinding-stone,' muttered the woman from Number Rat.

Her husband put the pot on it. She caught her breath.

'It resembles a human cranium,' said the woman from Number Hedgehog. 'Isn't it amusing?'

'Ho, absolutely!' cried her host, leaping back and putting his head on one side, critically. 'It sets off them three sets of red deer antlers a treat! Have you noticed how the different sizes are cunningly arranged on the wall to give the appearance of flapping into the distance?'

'Yes,' said the man from next door. 'We used to have a similar arrangement until she chucked 'em out. You know women. They see a thing all over everywhere, and right away they reckon it's common.'

'Oh, do they?' shouted his hostess, with unexpected vehemence. 'Well, how about this, then?'

Whereupon she snatched the lower antler from its peg, exposing the hitherto concealed buffalo and its scarlet addendum.

The woman next door reeled, and covered her eyes. Her husband leapt up.

'Come on, Spot!' he called, and pulled on the thong.

The further end of which came into the room with remarkably little resistance.

Everybody looked at the head.

An unseen child burped.

'He has eaten Spot!' shrieked the woman from Number Hedgehog. 'The little bastard has consumed our dog!'

'Ha!'

The neighbours swung round.

The woman from Number Rat was brandishing the cranial pot.

'It is no use giving yourself them airs, Lady Muck!' she cried. 'I would know this so-called present of yours any-where. It belonged to my poor dead dad.'

'I never claimed it was new,' snapped her neighbour. 'I purchased it second-hand from someone who doubtless came by it after your father's demise. Where did he keep it?'

'He kept it on the end of his neck!' shrieked the woman from Number Rat, and, snatching up the fallen antler, lashed hideously out.

The man from Number Rat sat in the middle of his new path, watching the moon rise. Smoke blew past him from the cave behind, and his nostrils flinched at the familiar fragrance. He had not chosen to prevent her. The apple did not fall far from the tree, and she would not waste good meat.

One day, they would have a proper garden here, with a pond. Possibly even a laburnum; they might well name their little home after it. It would be surrounded by other little homes, perhaps in crescents, like the moon, each separated from the other by a trim hedge. Everyone would be very nice to everyone else. It would all be terribly civilized.

The man smiled to himself, in the darkness. It was nice to have something to believe in.

Thanks for the Memory

The President has agreed to make available notes he made during the White House discussions on the arms sale to Iran. The notes are those the President takes to help him write his memoirs. At the end of the day, he writes down his impressions of the day's events, the people he has met and what he thought of them, and the decisions that were taken.

The committee investigating the Iran affair believes the notes will make clear the President's position.

The Times

MONDAY EVENING

Dear Diary,
Today was a real hard day.

It started off where I ate a little house. I did not know I had ate a little house until I found a little elf in my spoon. First off, I thought it was a roach, but when I looked on the back of the pack it said this was my lucky day because each Grape Nuts pack contained a little elf and a little house, and what you did was you put the little elf in the little house and then you would have a little house with a little elf in, and you could add it to your collection. When I found the little elf in my spoon I tipped all the Grape Nuts on to the table but there was no little house.

I guess I will have to go into Bethesda Naval and have the little house taken out. Otherwise my collection will look dumb, just a little elf standing next to a little witch and a little dragon and a little goblin and not in his little house.

George Shultz came in right after breakfast.

Here is the conversation:

'Good morning, Mr President.'

'I ate the little house, George.'

'Good. I think we should go up to the meeting now.'

18

The meeting was a tough meeting. Here are my notes:

As you look at the back of Caspar Weinberger's envelope, Iran is on the right and is joined to Iraq on the left. They are written down Ira**N** and Ira**Q** so we all know exactly who's who, because they are both of them followers of Islam, a camel-driver, but George says don't worry, anybody could get confused, and I should look at the photographs of an Ira**Q**i and an Ira**N**i in my update file.

Here is the conversation:

Me: 'They both look kind of Jewish, George.'
Weinberger: 'What did the President say, George?'
Shultz: 'He said they both look kind of Jewish.'
Weinberger: 'Okay. Just checking.'

The discussion opened up right after that, and I formed the impression that Ira**Q** and Ira**N** are different kinds of Islams and are fighting a war due to this, and the object is to get right to the other side of Weinberger's envelope. I also formed the impression, at 11.20 approximately Eastern Standard Time, that I had got the mango Danish.

Here is the conversation:

Shultz: '– or, alternatively, laundered through Tel Aviv?'
Me: 'Who ordered the mango Danish?'
Meese: 'What?'
Me: 'This seems to be a mango Danish. I ordered a blueberry muffin.'
Weinberger: 'I have your muffin, Mr President.'
Me: 'Then you get the mango Danish, am I right?'
Weinberger: 'I was the pretzel.'
Shultz: 'I have the pretzel. I ordered the cinammon toast.'
Meese: 'I have the cinammon toast. I ordered the mango Danish.'
*Me: 'Great! Now, just to kind of re-cap, Ira**Q** is the flakies with the long black shirts, right?'*

In the afternoon session, Shultz brought up some kind of thing we signed one time about a worldwide embargo against arms sales to Ira**N**, due to where they took US hostages. Weinberger said that we ought to look at this in the light of the fact that it was now the Lebanon that had the US hostages. I said maybe we ought to bomb it again. They all looked at me.

Here is the conversation:

Weinberger: 'We never bombed the Lebanon, Mr President.'

Me: 'Horse feathers! Gimme a map. Okay, what's that under my pinkie?'
Shultz: 'Tripoli, Mr President.'
Me: 'Hardy-ha-ha! Tell me we didn't bomb the hell out of Tripoli!'
Shultz: 'You are pointing at Tripoli, Lebanon, Mr President. We bombed Tripoli, Libya.'
Weinberger: 'If I can return to the matter of the Hawk sales to . . .'

I went out to the john. I think the little house is wedged somewhere. It gave me time to think. So we hit the wrong Tripoli. We bombed the Tripoli that didn't have our hostages and we didn't bomb the Tripoli that did. Don't tell me it's an easy mistake, Diary, some of those Navy pilots are pulling down a hundred thousand plus.

Still, I guess it's lucky we didn't take out Tripoli, Iowa.

TUESDAY EVENING

Dear Diary,
I missed the rest of yesterday's afternoon session, but I guess you know that. I hope you enjoyed *The Flintstones*. What I don't understand is, when they go to the drive-in on their dinosaur, how come the movie they see is in colour? I remember when colour came in, it was 1935. This is just like the Tripoli screw-up. Details count.

George Shultz came in right after breakfast.
Here is the conversation:
'Good morning, Mr President.'
'Look, George, I got another little house out of the new Grape Nuts pack. I now have two little elfs. Should I have one little elf inside and one outside, or what?'
'I think we should go up to the meeting now.'

The meeting was even tougher than yesterday. Here are my notes:
This is the story so far, as I understand it. We are at war with IraN because of the hostages they took and so we are not going to give them any arms or let anybody else give them any arms, except that we are going to give them arms because we bombed the wrong Lebanon and so we are at peace with IraN for maybe a couple of weeks, but we will have to go to war with them again as soon as they have used

our arms to bomb the right Lebanon and get US hostages back, but any arms they have not used we are going to have to get back, in case we have to use them to bomb IraN if they start taking US hostages.

Also, nobody must find out, because the Soviets are supplying arms to IraN which we have condemned on the grounds that this is destabilizing the area and, as a neutral, we cannot allow IraN to fall into the Soviet orbit because that would mean it fell out of the US orbit and we have to be friendly to IraN because we are at war with it. Also, the Soviets are shipping arms to IraQ. I guess this must be because IraQ is holding Soviet hostages, but Shultz just looks at the ceiling when I ask this, clearly it is something he does not want minuted at this moment in time, it is a damned sensitive area.

I went out right after the summary on account of Edwin Meese got the wrong waffle and Weinberger found mayo on his BLT and Shultz said what the kitchen needed was authority at the highest level and nobody could do it better than me so why didn't I go straighten them out? I am a sucker for flattery, Diary, it's the way I'm made, I guess. Hollywood can do that to you. I got back kind of late due to where they had *The Price is Right* on in the kitchen. A guy, just an ordinary guy from Topeka, Kansas, guessed the price of a new hi-fi system right to the damned cent! Where do we get such men?

When I got back, Shultz was talking about sending arms to Israel.

Here is the conversation:

Me: *'Great play, George! Israel will zap Lebanon and get the US hostages, so we don't have to sell arms to Iran and screw up relations with anybody, right?'*
George: *'No, Israel will sell the arms to Iran.'*
Me: *'I thought they were enemies.'*
George: *'They are.'*
Me: *'How's the waffle, Ed?'*
Meese: *'Terrific, Mr President.'*

I looked out the window for a while. Weinberger was saying how the guy they were going to use as a go-between for Colonel Oliver North was Adnan Khashoggi. He is a Saudi-Arabian, so I guess that as a sworn enemy of both Israel and Iran, he is in an ideal position to help them.

After a couple of hours, I realized I did not know who this Colonel Oliver North was.

Here is the conversation:

Weinberger: 'He is the Marine officer who headed up the investigation into the Lebanon bombing. He led the hunt for those responsible.'

Me: 'Did he get the guys who hit the wrong Tripoli?'

Weinberger: 'Not that Lebanon bombing, Mr President. This was the Lebanon bombing in 1983 when the Lebanese killed 241 US Marines.'

Me: 'Holy Moly! You mean the Lebanese got the wrong Tripoli, too? Isn't it about time they changed the name before anybody else gets killed? How about Walnut Creek? I always thought Walnut Creek was a great name for a town. It sounds like a good, clean town, a good town to live in, a good place to raise your kids. I grew up in a town like that. It was called Dixon, Illinois. Nobody ever bombed Dixon, Illinois.'

Weinberger: 'That was a really terrific bacon-lettuce-and-tomato, Mr President. Nobody could have swung it in that kitchen like you swung it. I don't suppose you could, I mean I hate to ask, but, you know, talking makes me kind of hungry, and . . .'

Me: 'Say no more, old buddy. While I'm up, who needs more coffee?'

But here's the crazy thing, Diary. When I got back, the room was empty. I guess they moved to another room for security purposes. It was a smart thing to do, I never did find out where they went, which just goes to show how secure it was. I have a great team there!

George came by tonight to say he's fixed it for me to go into Bethesda Naval tomorrow to have the little house removed. He says it's worth ten poll points, minimum, and be sure and wave from my window right after. Maybe hold up the little house.

I asked him about that other thing, with the **Q** and the **N** and all that, and he said not to worry, it would all be taken care of.

For Fear of Finding Something Worse

Exactly why Nanny Barnes left the service of the Princess of Wales remains something of a mystery.

Daily Express

NORLAND PLAIN, Wiltshire, nine o'clock on a glacial January morning, a pewter sky and a razor wind, the sleet pitting the cheeks like birdshot and the hoar grass beneath our feet hostile as a fakir's mattress, yet incredibly, suddenly into our line of sight, at the double, in full pack, blue breath pluming in immaculately co-ordinated puffs from their scarlet cheeks, yomped, in unbroken Indian file, the First Training Battalion the Queen's Own Heavy Nannies.

'There is probably no finer sight on God's earth,' murmured, at my elbow, Nanny-Major Putney. A tear trembled on her lower lash, froze, fell, and clinked off the toecap of her sensible shoe.

'How far have they come?' I enquired.

'Nine miles,' replied Nanny-Major Putney. 'Equivalent, of course, to three circuits of Hyde Park. Carrying, as you can see, full backpack containing – Sar'nt-Nanny Mortlake?'

'Nappies, cotton, twelve,' barked Nanny Mortlake, 'nappy-liners, paper, ditto, formula bottles, filled, four, gripewater bottles, filled, two, strained vegetables, canned, six, rusks, dry, ten, dummies, rubber, two, bibs, pelican, two, bibs, flannel, two, sponges, wet, three, towels, dry, four, powder, talcum, two, blankets, cellular, two, potties, enamel, two, pandas, stuffed, two, rings, teething, two, and, of course, *The Lady*, this week's, one.'

'Astonishing!' I cried. 'Nine miles, in these conditions! I begin to understand why Nanny Barnes found the going too rough.'

'Nonsense!' snorted Nanny-Major Putney. 'Nanny Barnes took to the physical hardships like a duck to bath-time. Is that not so, Nanny Chiswick?'

23

'Apsley correct,' said Nanny Chiswick, to my left. She lowered her field-glasses, and, pausing only to spit on her handkerchief and scrub at my chin, continued: 'When it came to jolly old knees-brown time, Nanny Barnes was tickety-boo. Nanny Barnes passed out first in her obstacle class. I have seen Nanny Barnes go over a ten-foot junket-covered climbing-frame with a screaming brat under each arm, reassemble a standard issue twelve-pounder high-chair in seven-point-three seconds, crawl under two Volvos and a Golf to retrieve a half-strangled gerbil, and still have enough puff left for three choruses of *This Little Piggy*.'

'There you are!' cried Nanny-Major Putney, triumphantly. 'When Mister Weedy called, Nanny Barnes was not at home!'

The eighty brogues stamped rhythmically past, a hundred metres off. The ground shook, and, in anticipation of deperambulatored rusks, rooks rose cawing from the skeletal trees. They were to be disappointed. Instead, the forty prams wheeled right, reformed impeccably in line abreast, and charged on towards a distant building, leaving the lusty echo of *Teddy Bears' Picnic* by forty marching contraltos fading on the icy air.

'The Regiment,' said Nanny-Major Putney, thwacking her thigh with her swagger-rattle, 'has always sworn by the 1934 Dunkley. Sturdy, reliable, stable – do you know, I have watched a Dunkley following the Quorn across ploughed fields at racing shove and the infant never bounced higher than two feet?'

'Good heavens!' I exclaimed.

'When I was a young-un,' interjected the hitherto mute Nanny Isleworth, 'I once had the pleasure of pushing a Dunkley across the Duke of Dunswold's grouse moor on the Twelfth of August. At one point we took both barrels on our left flank-panel, and, do you know, it didn't even remove the enamel?'

'Astonishing,' I said. 'How, I wonder, was Nanny Barnes under fire? Could it perhaps have been that which broke her will to –'

'Fiddle-de-dee!' roared Nanny-Major Putney. 'When the poo-poo was coming down, Nanny Barnes was like a rock! I was with her at Cowdray Park on the day her little swine threw his golly on to the field during the final chukka. She took three mallet-swipes without breaking stride and still managed to cheer the winning goal.'

'As I understand it,' said Nanny Chiswick, 'she *was* the winning goal.'

'I think,' said Nanny-Major Putney, 'you gentlemen of the press will not find the explanation for Nanny Barnes's resignation to lie in any lack of bottle. OH, WELL STORMED, THE HEAVIES!' she shrieked, suddenly.

I craned into the sleet.

'That building,' explained Nanny Mortlake, pointing, 'is a training replica of Harrods. Its twenty doors have to be burst through simultaneously, two nannies to a door.'

'What then?' I asked.

'Once inside, they have to whizz round their allotted departments in under three minutes and get out again without killing anyone.'

'Important,' said Nanny Chiswick.

'Anyone important,' nodded Nanny Mortlake.

Crashes, screams, yoicks, drifted back on the wind.

'Nanny Barnes,' I pressed. 'Was unarmed combat not, perhaps, her strongest . . .'

'Nanny Barnes,' replied Nanny-Major Putney hotly, 'passed out first in her Nasty Man course.'

'Really?'

'We put her in,' explained Nanny Chiswick, 'against our toughest instructor, a six-foot-four, squash-tuned, fully-soused, Simulated Commodity Broker. He kicked down the door of Night Nursery Complex 14, grabbed her from behind as she was bending over to tuck in her little horror, and yelled: *How about a spot of num-num, Nanny?*'

'Good God!'

'Yes, they don't come much viler, even in Godalming.'

'What happened!'

'Nothing too terrible,' replied Nanny-Major Putney. 'The St John's Ambulance people found him crawling through Salisbury. When she left the course, we allowed her to keep his teeth. OH, WELL DONE!'

Smoke was rising from the distant building. I joined in the applause.

Nanny-Major Putney poked Nanny Mortlake.

'What's next?' she barked. 'European Theatre Combined Ops, is it?' She turned to me. 'You'll like this. We drop them into a simulated Dordogne converted farmhouse or mock-Meribel ski-chalet, we get the pairs of Parent-Instructors utterly blotto, and we leave the nannies to mop up the entire blooming –'

'Sorry, Nanny-Major,' said Nanny Mortlake. 'Today we have naming of parts.'

'Oh, fudgecakes!' muttered Nanny-Major Putney.

'I'm sorry?'

All the nannies stared at me. The chill suddenly deepened.

'He is clearly,' muttered Nanny Isleworth, 'unfamiliar with the greatest poem in the language.'

She cleared her throat.

Today we have Naming Of Parts. Yesterday
We had Daily Cleaning. And tomorrow morning,
We shall have What To Do After Big Jobs. But today,
Today we have Naming Of Parts.'

'Forgive me once again,' I wheedled, 'but what exactly is naming of parts?'

Rolling her eyes, Nanny-Major Putney jabbed her rattle towards the drilling ranks and replied:

'They come to us as innocent gels. When in due course they go off to their units, they may well encounter an infinite number of incomprehensible technical terms.'

'It is a bottyless pit,' murmured Nanny Mortlake.

'Quite,' said Nanny-Major Putney. 'To take just one random example, there are seventy-three synonyms for winkle alone, and more coming along every minute. Only the other day, a nanny posted to Runcorn wrote to me complaining that she had been called upon to powder a bertie. She did not have the faintest idea where to begin.'

'I see,' I said. 'Well, perhaps it was just such a communication failure that brought about the Barnes resignation. After all, on her own admission, the Princess of Wales is as thick as a –'

'Stop!' cried Nanny-Major Putney. 'No member of this regiment has ever cracked through parent-failure! Golly gosh almighty, there is no eventuality towards which their training is more rigorously directed!' She paused. The great frame shook. Terrible forces were, quite clearly, warring within that dedicated bosom. She lowered, at last, her voice. 'Uncles, however,' she muttered from trembling lips, 'uncles lie beyond their control. And when there are tears before bedtime, it is invariably to the pernicious influence of the uncle that we should look. Show me a decent gel driven to

26

the conclusion that a life in the Nannies is not for her and, nine times out of ten, I will show you a wrong uncle.'

A long silence followed, as things fell into place.

'You cannot mean,' I cried, 'Prince Ed –'

The Nanny-Major threw up a peremptory mitten. It held a mouth-sized bar of soap.

'Hush, hush!' she threatened. 'Whisper who dares!'

The Great Fire of Cricklewood

MARCH 1

Lord's day

BEING WEERY last night, with the companye opposite leeving late and they very gay and much disposed to banging doors and crying their fare-wells generously aloud to the Streete at large and one or two falling down among binns and the lids rolling; and I awakening and opening the sash to remonstrate kindly with them, and the sash, being insecure and the roapes rotted, coming down upon my Necke and the attendant agonie thereof setting my dear wife on a stir; and I, enjoyned by her to determine the source of a sound very like micturation against our *Magnolia*, descending with a Crickette Stump yet finding no one upon the dark step but milke bottels in several and they flying about at my advent; being, as I say, weery, I lay long a-bed: until nigh on 7 a.m., when the Paperboy, bearing so rich a plenitude of supplementes as to prevent their easy passage through our flappe, smote upon the knocker-plate with great ferocitie.

My wrath at which, upon opening to him, much diminished by his brandishing in my face a shoe, this cut aboute with bottle-shards, and enquiring in a common manner whether my opinion was that Plimsolles grew upon trees. Gave him *50p* for his grievance, and hee by God's good grace mollified.

Thus, *volens nolens*, up betimes and my dear wife volunteering to peruse the newspapers in my behalfe and vouchsafe unto me at our joint Leisure such small intelligences as therein contayned upon the matters of AIDS, Mrs Reagan and the Subjects mooted for *Mastermind* later in the day (these being the seeming-substaunce of the two hundred several pages), she observed that, since it was March 1 and the hoar lifted, I shoulde be better employed in seezing the opportunitie to transplante the *Berberis* about which she has been much on and on at me since October, it now so burgeoned as to threaten the *Photinia* and even, mayhap, the House itselfe; this latter being of a cunning modern structure eerily vulnerable to the sinewy roote.

Thence, in reasonable good hart despyte the sleete, to my Shedde; where, the door being stucke and the securing hooks ravaged by the winter damp, all the Tools detached themselves on a sudden and fortuitously fell upon me, several breaking with the ruste and thus haply facilitating my choyce.

Thither with a stoute spade to the *Berberis*, and to my Taske.

The *Berberis* proving, howsoever, to be so unprecedentedly flourished as to be now fast entwyned with the neighbour *Photinia*, incumbency required my advaunce into the depths of the latter in order to attacke the roote of the former.

But my hatte nocked off, and a sharp branche in the eer and another in the eye, and no room to swing the spade.

A repayre to the Shedde thus forced upon me, to retrieve a pruning-hooke and sheers wherewith to excise a small redoubt within the *Photinia* whence to lay attacke to Monsieur Barberry. But at my first lunge at the upper fortifications of the *Photinia*, a great shuddre to the Wristes and the pruning-hooke stuck fast! Upon tugginge same, the haft detached itselfe; I looked at it for some considerable time, the fine drizzel dropping.

At last, and in my rage, fell to furiously with the sheers, clumpes of verdure flying on every side, and made myself a hole; not, by God's great blessing, in myselfe, but in the bushe; and thus ensconced, sette to upon the *Berberis* roote.

After an half-hour, many a lygament broke and eyes full of Spottes, much of the bush was up; but the rootes revealed to be stretching out beneeth the Fencinge.

To my left Neighbour; he bleer and wretched, his night apparently much disturbed by Oafs breaking bottels. We agreed upon the sad plummeting of the Countrie into roguerie and mayhem. Divining his distresse, I did not presse my suit anent the diggynge-up of his Garden, lest (it was suddenly borne in upon me) my roote be observed to have penetrated the foundations of his own lodgings.

Home agayne, and naught for it but to hack free the rootes, this necessitating the chopping down of a *Ceanothus* to which, in faith, I had not been much partial these seven years, it having low cover and thus, to my mind, persuading Catts of its literally privy propensities.

To work with the Ax, it leaping about lively enough, the *Ceanothus* trunk being wette and springey; so thence, in due course, to the House at the runne, holding my thum with my good hand that it should not spirt, and calling to my dear wife for some manner of Plaster.

But she, descending in haste from her Chamber, straight-way set up a great wailing – despyte my earnest Assurances that the wound was but a nicke – and would not be consoled; poynting instead through the Window to where the *Ceanothus* lay.

It immediately transpiring that she had become en-amoured of the ghastlie Thing, I made haste to bind my thum myselfe, deploying my teeth to much deft effect, informing her hastily the whiles of the fearful Diseese which I had, with breaking hart, observed upon the leefs, thereat determining upon an instant and merciful despatch to spare the dear Bush further suffring.

Sensing in her – for what is the ideal marital state, if not that Bliss which proceeds onlie from true mutual under-standing? – an urgent desire for boots (wherewith to investigate the grislie blight for herselfe), I forthwith excused myselfe and hurried back to the Spott, trusting to conflagrate the evidence, on the grounds, if challenged, of scourging the great Plague at source ere it spread and engulfed us all!

To the bon-fire site, lugging the *Ceanothus* and the *Photinia* wreckage; these, in their trail, beheading our one crocus, the splinting of which with a sliver of Bam-bu (cunningly concealed so as to be invisible from the House) cost precious seconds.

Yet worse, the wetness of the foliage and the prevaling damp of the Ayre proving inimical to the match, a great Terror stole upon me that the corpse would not merely lie,

30

like great Caesar, its wounds so many poor dumb mouths speeking for me – nay, speeking *of* me – to anyone in boots who chose, through which malevolent Suspicion or that I neither knew nor cared, to trudge thither; but also (such are the dire conceits which mischievous Fancy visits upon the over-schooled) would appear, this time like poor butchered Banquo, some evening at our dining-table: a ceanothine Ghost, glowering at me across the tureens, while, upon my right, the sweet Mother of my children slipped, at her arboreal loss, slowly into madnesse.

And so (this thought palpably lying beyond all entertaining) to Shedde: wherein, by the Almighty's ever-forgiving charity, a can of petroleum spirit whilom left to serve the mower's need now fell readily to hand; and I was able, in a trice, to empty, upon the bushie torment of my conscience, the igneous balm.

Arriving soon thereafter back at the House – having paused in the boiler-room only long enough to wash a strange blackness from my face and divest myselfe of Galoshes which, being of a clearly inferior varietie, had unaccountably melted – and fully expecting some ribald note to be made concerning the whereabouts of my hair and eye-browes, discovered instead my dear Children much exercised about a great fire they had observed sweeping the Neighbourhood.

So I rose, and went to the window; and observed to my beloved wife that I thought it to be on the back-side of Finchley Road, started perhaps by some incautious baker who had chosen to ignore Our Lord's injunction as to His day, in the service of greed.

She, for her part, expressed some reservation concerning this; in that the Inferno seemed to have chosen as its seat our own back fence, a spott customarily devoid of bakeries, and had thence spread outwards to inflict upon our neighbour's previously impressive cedars a fate which she – it subsequently proved correctly – divined to be the source of insensate shrieking from the propertie next door.

Ever a fellow for whom communitie preceded self, I sprang on the very instant from the House, recalling that, somewhere in my trusty Shedde, there lay a hose which it would be the work of a moment to connect, once I had onlie lain my hands upon the thing with which one connected it, leaving the dear companion of my bed and destiny to call up the Fire Brigade; who, I assured her, would readily endorse my observation that it was a meteorological fact too well-known to merit any argument that spring lightning could strike, without a second's warning, in any place and at any time.

Sea Change

A public beach has been put out of bounds at Great Yarmouth so that fifty pairs of little terns can nest in peace. A stretch of shore a third of a mile long and a hundred yards wide has been cleaned and roped off.

The terns have flown 4,000 miles from Gambia to mate.

Daily Telegraph

'I CAN remember when you couldn't get on that beach without a tie,' said the crab, from the edge of the rock-pool.

The gull, perched on the ledge above it, glanced down.

'Must have been a bugger to knot,' it observed, 'with claws.'

One stalked eye emerged slowly from the crab's armoured slot and stared at the gull for a time.

'What?' it said.

'Bow tie, was it?' enquired a prawn, breaking the surface. 'I couldn't help hearing.'

'It would have to be,' said the gull. 'He could hardly wear the other sort.'

'I've always wondered what they were called,' said the prawn, thoughtfully. 'Has it ever struck you as funny, having one called a bow and the other one not called anything?'

'No, it hasn't,' said the gull.

The crab's other eye came out.

'Why would he have to wear a bow, anyway?' asked the prawn.

'First off,' said the gull, 'it would go better with his shape. But mainly, it's the practical side. If he wore the other kind of tie, it would trail in the mud.'

'It would be filthy,' nodded the prawn, 'in no time. I see that.'

'Plus trip him up. It is one of the shortcomings of running sideways. The tie would hang down in front,' explained the gull, 'and he would be forever running over it.'

33

'Unless he had the knot on one side,' said the prawn.

'He'd look ridiculous,' said the gull.

The prawn considered this.

'Beats me why they wanted him to wear a tie at all,' it said.

'They were probably partial,' murmured a winkle who had hitherto kept itself to itself, 'to a nice bit of dressed crab!'

At which it convulsed so uncontrollably as to lose its grip on the underside of the rock, drop to the sand, and roll about, hooting.

'*Nice bit of dressed crab!*' it shrieked. 'Where do I get 'em from!'

The gull rose on a single flap, sank smartly to the beach, and put a yellow claw on the winkle.

'Shall I do us all a favour?' it enquired.

'Leave it out,' said the winkle, muffled. 'It is not as if I can help myself. It is in the blood, if you are a winkle. Generations of salty Cockney wit etcetera. It is expected of us. Also, being cheery goes with ending up on a pin. Look at World War One. Nil carborundum and so forth. Gassed last night, and gassed the night before. *Are we downhearted?* No!'

'Oh, let him go,' said the crab, wearily. 'It is the oldest joke in the book.'

'*I* laughed,' said the prawn.

'It's the way I tell 'em,' said the winkle.

The gull resumed its perch.

'I still don't understand,' it said, 'where they expected you to get a tie from.'

The crab sighed. Bubbles winked on its terrible jaws.

'Not *me*,' it said. 'They did not expect *me* to wear a tie. They

expected one another to wear 'em. The men wore sponge-bag trousers and striped blazers and panama hats, and the women wore long frocks and bonnets with daisies on, it was all very elegant, this beach.'

'Pull this one,' said the prawn, 'they would have gone down like bricks.'

'They did not wear 'em in the water,' said the crab, rolling each eye independently. 'Don't you know anything? When they wanted to swim, they went inside these little hut efforts, and they changed into bathing suits, and someone pushed the huts into the water, and they got out of the back door and into the sea.'

'Stone me!' cried the prawn. 'What a palaver! It's not even

as if they eat plankton. They just go in and lollop about a bit and then they come out and turn red. Fancy going to the expense of a hut!'

The crab sighed.

'You had to be there,' it murmured. 'It had a lot of charm. It had innocence. They used to bring ukuleles and butterfly nets. They used to play French cricket and sing *My Old Man Said Follow the Van*. They did not,' muttered the crab darkly, 'have nude beaches. They did not,' and here he waved a gnarled claw towards the roped enclosure, 'have subsidized mating.'

'Oh, look!' cried the winkle, as the others, on the crab's signal, stared.

'What is it?' said the gull.

'She's having one of her terns!' shrieked the winkle.

The prawn fell about.

'You may laugh,' said the crab, 'but it is not only a gross affront to decency, it is a wanton misuse of council money. Little terns com:ng over here, having it away on the rates.'

'I wonder why we never see any great terns,' said the gull.

'He's right, you know,' said the winkle. 'Remember Jimmy James? Jewell and Warriss? Remember Wilson, Keppel and Betty? They all played here once. I blame television.'

'*Great turns!*' howled the prawn, clutching itself octapodally. 'You are a caution, and no mistake! Have you ever thought of doing it professionally yourself?'

The winkle shook its shell.

'It's a terrible life, these days,' it replied. 'All they want is smut. Or impressions of Robin Day. Not easy, if you happen to be a mollusc. Besides, very few of 'em speak winkle.'

'It would not surprise me,' said the crab, 'if there was not a ban on tern jokes. They have, after all, flown here from Gambia. It would not surprise me if making tern jokes was punishable under the Race Relations Act.'

'I wonder why they don't do it at home?' enquired the gull. 'Fancy flying halfway round the world for a bit of wing-over! I usually manage with a lump of driftwood. It's a bad day for me if I have to go further than fifty feet.'

'They come over here,' replied the crab bitterly, 'on account of it is the life of Riley. Roped-off beach, no cats, no tar, no donkey doings, RSPB patrols, nothing to do all day except –'

'– take terns!' said the winkle. 'Sorry, sorry, slipped out!'

'In all probability,' said the gull, 'they do not even have to build anything. They probably get a council nest. They probably go straight to the top of the list. Fly in, make your clawprint in the space provided, ten minutes later you are –'

'– going for a quick tern along the beach!'

'I'd write all these down,' gasped the prawn, 'if the tide wasn't coming in.'

'It would not surprise me,' muttered the gull, 'if they did not even have to be married. It is probably an offence to ask 'em. You know councils. Give 'em half a chance to be seen doing sunnink for the single-parent egg, and before you know it they are coming round with a red-checked tablecloth and a candle in a bottle and a hot lugworm dinner with all the trimmings.'

'They look after their own, all right,' muttered the crab. 'Bloody clever, these Communists.'

'Sharp left terns,' said the winkle.

The prawn fell back, waving its pleopods feebly.

'Lucky I haven't got ribs,' it wheezed, 'I'd be strapped up by now!'

'They just come to me,' explained the winkle. 'Call it a gift.'

'You could've made a fortune in saucy postcards,' said the prawn warmly, when it had recovered, 'with the right contacts.'

'I've never understood why they're supposed to be saucy,' said the winkle. 'They're usually about the ones with hair under their noses asking the ones with two lumps on the front if they would care for a nice big winkle. What's so saucy about that?'

'Not just Communists, either,' said the gull, darkly. 'A fair number of 'em are gay. That is what attracts councils more than anything, these days.'

'There's a big ternover,' said the winkle.

'Is there no end to his repertoire?' cried the prawn.

'Bottomless,' replied the winkle.

They both fell over.

'I can remember,' said the crab, 'when what councils spent their money on was deckchairs and bandstands and lifebelts and little lights on the lamp-posts and stopping piers from rotting and men going round with spikes picking rubbish up off the sand. What is it all coming to?'

'It is probably a symbol of something,' said the gull. 'A lot of things are, these days.'

36

'Where will it all end?' asked the prawn.
'In moral depravity, is where,' said the crab.
'Tern to page three,' said the winkle.

Maybe It's Because I'm a Landowner

Who knows? Why not just say the times call forth the man, and leave it at that?

It may be that I commended myself to them by the sobriety of my neckwear, the conservatism of my topiary, the meticulousness of my VAT returns, the brevity of my sideburns, the unturbulence of my marriage, or the egglessness of my waistcoat, but the reasons for their choice are, surely, secondary to the choice itself?

As far as I am concerned, when the London Residuary Body comes round in the middle of the night with a civic challenge, a six-figure murmur, and the promise of an OBE if the nose is kept spotless for its allotted span, mine is not to reason why.

The London Residuary Body, for those of you who thought that a seven-man quango was either a mediaeval Wiltshire game involving staves or an arcane dance routine that perished with Edmundo Ros, is the genteel *Waffenkommando* which took over London on All Fools' Eve, charged with sweeping up the detritus left by Ken Livingstone's newt-pack and turning the metropolis back into a land fit for Eros.

It is run by Sir Godfrey Taylor, and, as befits a citizen who in his brief span as the Chairman of the Southern Water Authority became known as the Father of Modern Pipework, it was he himself who arrived at my spotless suburban premises last Monday evening and personally made me the offer only a base ingrate would have refused.

I am to be London's new Cultural Supremo. As the refugee lines of bisexual mummers and provisional vegans and handicapped windsurfers and Rastafarian steeplejacks trundle their subsidized hardcarts away from County Hall and into the outer darkness, a civic void has been created into which a man of impeccable middle-class credentials is required to step.

My brief is simple: to establish across-the-board support and funding for all those valiant underprivileged minorities who have been out in the socialist cold for so long, and whose turn it now is to march into the broad sunny uplands of the new Jerusalem. I have therefore cobbled together a short working paper: it takes the form of question and answer, in the hope that Londoners will thus be stimulated to send in enquiries of their own. My door is ever open.

WILL THERE BE STREET THEATRE?

It is one of my top priorities. Within mere minutes of my appointment, I had established the Michael Denison and Dulcie Gray Thespian Ensemble, whose itinerant marquee will be offering a full programme of experimental modern drama including *Dear Octopus*, *French without Tears*, *The Second Mrs Tanqueray*, and – provided there is not too great a puritan outcry – *When We are Married*. They have also commissioned a morally uplifting three-acter which will play Brixton this autumn, entitled *The Darkies of Wimpole Street*.

Nor have more down-to-earth tastes been neglected. The Donald Sinden Fol-de-Rols will tour working-class areas with a full programme of jocular monologues, Cockney songs and farmyard impersonations, while a necessary concession to alternative theatre has been made in the shape of the Nicholas Parsons One, which will play the Greater London roundabouts with a programme of slightly off-colour golf stories recited from the back of an open Armstrong Siddeley.

THERE WILL OF COURSE BE INDOOR THEATRE AS WELL?

There will of course be indoor theatre as well. For example, the Round House will be turned over exclusively to the White Arts, a full repertoire of cultural events committed to the celebration of white pride, from cake-icing, cable-stitching and floral-clockplanting to olde tyme dancing, raffia-work and Rover-polishing. There will be a permanent exhibition of garden gnomes in the foyer, weekly son-etlumière Gang Shows in the car park and, on major annual festivals such as Father's Day and Mrs Thatcher's Wedding Anniversary, harmonium-accompanied recitals of new greetings-card verses by top-name Anglican sidesmen.

BUT THE NATIONAL AND THE NFT WILL CONTINUE TO GET AWAY WITH ALL SORTS OF INCOMPREHENSIBLE FOREIGN AND SUBVERSIVE MUCK, WON'T THEY?

I'm glad you asked that. The short answer is that, thanks to the so-called Arts so-called Council chucking it about like a drunken sailor, they will undoubtedly try it on; but they will not get away with it. Fortunately, the administration of the buildings themselves falls within the LRB fief, and since it will be up to me to decide whether or not some crackpot Jap film full of little shrieking sadists constitutes a fire-hazard, or whether or not five hours of nude gobbledegook from the Howard Brenton Ad Hoc Solidarity Tarts Collective is likely to lead to a breach of the peace, I very much doubt that Johnny Intellectual is going to have things all his own way!

I have, as a matter of fact, already set in train a Cecil Parker Retrospective for the NFT, but I have not yet quite decided whether it is to be *Floradora* at the Cottesloe and *Alf's Button* at the Olivier, or vice-versa.

CAN YOU REASSURE US ABOUT THE MUSICAL SCENE?

Let me reassure you about the musical scene. Similar guidelines to the above will apply at major venues such as the Festival Hall, Albert Hall, Wigmore Hall, and so on, viz. any attempt at atonal, aleatory, serial, or other cacophonic garbage from the likes of Webern, Stockhausen, Cage, and the rest of their modish tin-eared breed will be met with an immediate air-raid warning giving audiences five minutes to clear the premises. Anyone attempting to applaud the siren will be charged with insulting behaviour and fined on the spot.

We fully expect that the musical world will rapidly come to its senses and realize which side its subsidy is buttered. I have laid down plans for a South Bank season of Mantovani's Greatest Hits (*arr. V. Doonican*), and the Purcell Room is being hung with castanets, bulls' heads and plastic pineapples in preparation for the permanent residence of Troyes and His Chamber Mandoliers (*Shirley Abicair, zith.*).

In homage to England's greatest tenor, all ticket booths will henceforth be known as websters.

PROGRESSIVE JAZZ?

Certainly. The New Squadronaires are even now being fitted out with roguish pink tuxedos, and earnest attempts are being made to resuscitate Eve Boswell.

WHAT PLANS FOR WORKSHOPS?

Extensive ones. Cultural self-development being a prime field of LRB operations, I have already drawn up a list of citizen-involvement groups which will produce a creative flowering not seen since the great days of Bakelite, Vic Oliver and the lovat plus-four.

Already eagerly under way are the Kings Cross Respectable Matrons Jams and Jellies Collective, the Hendon Fair Isle Cardigan Workshop, the Sutton & Cheam Heterosexuals for Real Suet Campaign Committee, the Palmers Green & Southgate Paint the Skirtings Eau-De-Nil Artists Co-operative, the Cricklewood Motor Mower and Strimmer Discussion Group, the Whetstone Spinsters for a Nuclear Rich Zone Literary Society, the Knightsbridge Raised Investment Consciousness Circle, and the Hampstead & Highgate Ad Hoc Slap the Children Fund Marching Band.

AND WILL THERE STILL BE A NOTTING HILL CARNIVAL?

Absolutely! Catering for the self-expression of minority groups must ever be at the forefront of the LRB commitment. The Notting Hill Carnival will thus become the Holland Park Carnival, a colourful annual event providing not only a long-neglected outlet for the natural high spirits of merchant bankers, media executives, cocoa brokers, vanity publishers, and many such cultural subgroups, but also a big draw for tourists keen to watch natives dressed up in their amusing Calvin Klein finery and foxtrotting in the streets.

Generous LRB help will be given in setting up ethnic spotted dick and baccarat stalls, and the Metropolitan Police, I am sure, may safely be relied upon to take off their helmets, throw their regulation dignity to the winds, and guess the weight of Lady Antonia Pinter's cake. I also expect a blind eye to be turned on the substances which these simple folk sniff as part of their social rituals.

In the evening, there will be BMW races in Clarendon Road, traditional breadroll-throwing and cork-shooting in Norland Square, and, after dinner, a torchlight procession to the top of Campden Hill to watch the lobster thermidor come up.

**THANK YOU FOR LISTENING.
ALL FURTHER ENQUIRIES AND SUGGESTIONS
MAY BE ADDRESSED TO ME
c/o THE DENNIMARGE BANQUETING SUITE,
COUNTY HALL, LONDON SE1**

Cloud Cuckoo Land

Dear Sir,
In all this Chernobyl business, is there a bright side to look on?

Petrified, Wisbech

Dear Petrified,
Yes. The bright side to look on is that nobody knew where Kiev was before. Millions of us have now been able to locate Kiev on the map. Discovering a new fact every day is a plus. I think that more or less sums up the bright side. We have also learned, of course, that graphite melts, which is another fact we probably did not know before, but since that is only about 25% bright side, I do not in all honesty feel we can look on it.

Dear Sir,
I live next door to Petrified, and she has just come in with your reply. I think she feels a little better, although she is still worried about growing another head. As you rightly say, I did not know where Kiev was before, I had only heard of it as Chicken Kiev, which is a leg full of stuff that squirts on to your tie when you stick a fork in it. What I should like to know is whether it is still safe to eat?

G. F. Noles, Wisbech

Dear Mr Noles,
I am not entirely clear as to your question. Do you want to know if it's safe to eat things off your tie? If so, it rather depends on the tie. Some materials in foreign ties, synthetic fibres, dyes, and so forth *are* harmful, but I must stress that British ties have to conform to the most rigorous safety standards, and there has never, to my certain knowledge,

been an accident involving a British tie. The Government would have told us.

If, on the other hand, you are enquiring as to whether it is safe to eat Chicken Kiev, the short answer is: not in Kiev. It should be safe to eat it in Wisbech, however, although that may depend to some extent on prevailing wind conditions. Your safest course would be to stick your fork in and wait to see what happens to your tie. If it rots and drops off, I should send it back and ask the waiter to bring you something tinned.

Dear Sir,
I live across the road from G. F. Noles, who is running up and down the street waving your letter, it is the first time he has been in print and there will be no living with him now, he is a cocky little sod at the best of times, and I should just like to register my protest at your printing his name, because everybody will now be able to identify Petrified as the lady next door, and this could well upset the Russians in the event of them following up this bomb of theirs with an invasion.
I think you ought to know that I have spoken to Shaken Rigid up the road, and he says there were men on Wisbech Station this morning with snow on their boots.
Bloody Furious, Wisbech

Dear Bloody Furious,
I have not yet heard from Shaken Rigid, but he seems to be quite hysterical! The accident in Kiev was not a bomb at all. I ask you, is it likely the Russians would go around bombing their own nuclear power plants?

Dear Sir,
Yes, and I'll tell you for why. It is just the sort of devious effing caper they would get up to, any minute now they will start screaming sabotage, it is all a plot to give them an excuse to launch World War III, I speak as I find.
Still, you're the last person I have to tell about disinformation, am I right? When Bloody Furious came in just now with your letter, I noticed your attempt to persuade him that I am masquerading as Shaken Rigid. Typical.
Quite Hysterical, Wisbech

Dear Quite Hysterical,
Forgive me, there seems to have been a misunderstanding. I shall be writing to Shaken Rigid under separate cover, but let me first attempt to alleviate your fears by saying that I find wholly preposterous your suggestion that Russia is acting as an *agent provocateur* in this unfortunate episode. It would be entirely uncharacteristic of their current stance.

Dear Sir,
I am glad you know so much about Russians, my friend Quite Hysterical says you ought to be on *Mastermind*, Professor Dickhead from London answering questions on How You Can Believe Every Single Word Those Mad Buggers Say, 1917-1987. If you know so much, perhaps you would be good enough to inform me how much radioactive rain has to fall into Finnish rivers before it affects the trees they use in newspapers and I start having Siamese twins from reading the *Sun*. It is bad enough the way the print comes off already, my husband had the whole of Samantha Fox's left buttock on his shirt yesterday, how long will it be before I have to start burning his dungarees?

Petrified, Wisbech

Dear Petrified,
I thought you were supposed to be feeling a little better. I thought you weren't worrying about anything except the possibility of a second head.

Dear Sir,
Yes, well, she's met us all in the pub since then, and she's a nervous bloody wreck now, what with all your prevarications etcetera, you are like that dalek Macdonald during the Falklands thing, there is no reason to panic, there is plenty of condensed milk to go round etcetera etcetera, well, we of the Hands Off Wisbech Ad Hoc Solidarity Committee would not trust you further than we could throw you.

You have still not sent me the letter under separate cover, as promised in yours of the ultimo to Quite Hysterical; what's the matter, sunshine, has something come to your notice, i.e. further reports of snow on boots,

parachutists on Hampstead Heath, meter maids suddenly turning signposts round, people asked to collect saucepans, railings, etcetera?

Anyway, it does not necessarily have to be the Russians who blew it up, it could well have been Gaddafi, they are everywhere, Libyans, I know for a fact they are up Russia in droves learning sabotage, it could be they reckon that by blowing up Kiev they will, what's the word, precipitate international confrontation, also drive up oil prices as the result of decent people tearing down nuclear power plants with their bare hands, before you know it Esso will be six quid a gallon.

It would not surprise me if Scargill had a hand in it somewhere, he is a well-known Russian agent.

Shaken Rigid, Wisbech

Dear Shaken Rigid,
Scargill?

Dear Sir,
I write on behalf of Shaken Rigid, who has gone off to the gents foaming at the mouth, and I must say we of the Wisbech Fight Ivan on the Beaches Hope and Glory Collective fully sympathize with him.

Do not tell us you have not considered the possibility of all this being a plot by the International Marxist Conspiracy to re-open uneconomic pits. Pull this one, it has got bells on.

By the way, we have just switched on the weather forecast again and that little nerd with the pebble glasses is chortling away about isobars and troughs and so forth, why can't they speak English, why can't they tell us which way this cloud is blowing, I have got £1,400 in the Abbey National, and they require seven days' notice of withdrawal in writing. If I am going to be irradiated, I intend splashing it out on big women, but if the cloud blows the other way, I do not want to forfeit a month's interest, as I shall continue saving up for a new Montego.

There is also the question of my loft extension, I have put on two undercoats and it is fiddling work, is there any point finishing off in top-quality gloss, if it is all going to flake off anyway due to nuclear sleet light to variable coming from the east later in the day and an unexpected

**warm front removing the tiles? Why can't those meteoro-
logical bastards be straight with us, is this why I pay £58
per annum?**

Choked, Wisbech

Dear Choked,
I have had quite enough of all this. How incredible it is that
we should be concerning ourselves here with an incident in a
far-away country involving people of whom we know
nothing!

And while you're up, shut the window.

The Revised Version

from GENESIS

. . . beast of the earth, and to every fowl of the air, and to everything that creepeth upon the earth, wherein *there is* life, I *have given* every green herb for meat: and it was so. 31 And God saw everything that he had made, and, behold, *it was* very good. And the evening and the morning were the sixth day.

2 THUS the heavens and earth were finished, and all the host of them.
2 And on the seventh day God ended his work which he had made; and he was about to rest on the seventh day from all his labours, when he looked again at every thing that he had made, and, behold, *it was* not quite as good as he had thought. For some of the coving *that there* was in that place had come away, nor was there a host of shelving; also there were bubbles in the wallpaper, and a drip from somewhere.
3 And God said, I was about to bless the seventh day and sanctify it, because I had planned to have *a bit of* a lie in and rest from the work which I had created and made, but plastering will not do itself, there is no peace for, there is no peace for, it will come to me in a minute.
4 And the LORD God said, I wonder if there is anywhere open?
5 But there was not anywhere open.
6 Therefore the LORD God formed man *of the* dust of the ground, and breathed into his nostrils the breath of life; and man became a living soul.
7 And the LORD God

planted a garden centre eastward in Eden, and adjacent *to it* in that place set he a homecare mart; and there he put the man that he had formed.

8 And the LORD God went back to make a list.

9 And behold, in the fullness of time, God went again to that place and called unto Adam and said unto him, Where art thou?

10 And Adam cried unto the LORD God, saying, I am out back stacking PVC guttering, I cannot be everywhere at once unlike some people I could mention, I have only got one pair of hands.

11 Whereat the LORD Customer waxed exceeding wroth, saying: if thou art not satisfied with the hands that I have made thee, that can be fixed; and while I am at it, perhaps I will throw in a trunk and a couple of antlers.

12 And Adam came out quickly from that place where he was.

13 And he spake unto the LORD God, saying, Can I be of any assistance?

14 And God said, here is my list.

15 But when the man looked at the list, he straightway *smote* himself upon the brow, crying, I can do the half-inch Yorkshire joints, the eau-de-nil undercoat is always *in*

stock, the Polyfilla is no problem, we are up to here with ready-pasted Vymura, but I can not do the two-inch pre-cast coving. There is no call *for* two-inch pre-cast coving.

16 And God spake in a voice like thunder, crying, I am the LORD thy God and I have set thee above all the beasts of the field, never mind all the builders requisites; if I call for two-inch pre-cast coving, is there not a call for it?

17 And Adam thought apart awhile, and replied in this wise, saying: it is possible that it is out back somewhere, we only opened this morning, I have not yet taken stock; if the LORD my God would care to hang on a minute, I shall see what I can do.

18 But God spoke unto him again, saying: The LORD thy God is not in the habit of hanging on, I shall find thee a help meet for thee.

19 And the LORD God caused a great sleep to fall upon Adam, and he slept: and he took *one of* his ribs, and closed up the flesh instead thereof.

20 And the rib, which the LORD God had taken *from* the man, made he a woman, and brought her unto the man.

21 And Adam cried aloud, saying: where did he come

from?

22 And God replied, I have fashioned a rib *to be* thy assistant, and make the tea.

23 And Adam said, truly thou art a fantastic handy-god, O LORD, thou hast done a remarkable job in the time, despite the odd structural flaw.

24 And God said, it is a woman.

25 Whereat Adam marvelled, crying: If I could get a couple of gross of ribs *from* somewhere, they could be a very big seller.

26 But to the woman, he spake in this wise, saying: nip out back, Sid, and see if we have got any lengths *of* two-inch pre-cast coving.

27 And they were both naked, the man and the woman, and they were not ashamed.

3 AND God took from the man all that had been *on his* list, and went away from that place and set to work speedily, for it was almost noon on the seventh day and there were many cracks to be made good due to settlement, and much paper to hang, and a great *deal* of shelving to be put up; and many sashcords had already perished, and subsidence had caused many doors to stick so hard *that* the LORD God

had to remove the hinges.

2 And some of the screws rolled under cupboards where even the LORD God could not reach them.

3 And much of the glass that he had brought with him to that place was one millimetre larger than he had measured and shattered *when* he tried to force it in.

4 And however much paper of whichever pattern he had brought back from Eden, and no matter which room he was papering, he found that he was always one roll short.

5 And no matter which shade of emulsion the LORD God put on, it was invariably just a tiny bit darker than it had looked on the colour chart.

6 Or a tiny bit lighter.

7 And God grew great in his anger, crying: I have made the giraffe and the orchid; lo! I have fashioned the spider and the snowflake and the jellyfish after their wondrous fashion, I even did that duck-billed thing with the flat feet for a laugh, and all was as a piece of cake, compared with this. Yea, though I go back a bit, mind, was the Milky Way not knocked up in the twinkling of an eye, and everything fitted? How, then, shall it be that with this that I do now *there is* never enough of anything even

though there was more than enough at the beginning, or, if there is, it is always a bit different from anything else?

8 But there was no answer to that.

9 And God said, I wonder if they are still open?

10 And he took *his* new list, and he returned eastward to Eden, and behold, they were still open.

11 And the LORD God went in unto them; and a bell had been put above the door, and it jangled.

12 And God made a murmuring in the wind, saying: what is it, that they have need of a bell? And he called unto Adam, and said unto him, Where art thou this time?

13 And lo! a voice came *from* afar, crying: Be with you in a minute, due to where we are up to our eyes stocktaking.

14 Yet the LORD God did not wax wroth upon this occasion, for he believed truly that the man was going about his business; and he saw that it was good to do so, for it was the seventh day, and it was *as* it should be.

15 But after much time passed, the LORD God began to wax ever so slightly irritable, for there was a host of plumbing still to be plumbed, and rodding-out to do in great measure; and

he had still not even so much as touched the garden.

16 Yet the irritation was as nothing to his wroth when Adam and his assistant came at last to that place *where he* was; for they were both clad in long brown warehouse coats.

17 And the LORD God spake unto them through his teeth, saying: well?

18 And the man said, I heard thy voice in the garden centre, and I was afraid, because I *was* naked; and I hid myself.

19 And God said: I?

20 And Adam said, all right, we.

21 And God said, Who told thee that thou *wast* naked? Hast thou eaten of the tree, whereof I commanded thee that thou shouldest not eat?

22 And Adam replied saying: Sid said we should, she said we ought to taste the stock, they could be a duff consignment of apple trees, we might be taking money under false pretences; am I right, Sid?

23 But the woman answered him not; and looked at her nails.

24 And the LORD God cried unto Adam, saying: I gave thee the seventh day to run a nice little business, that it would keep thee out of mischief, but thou hast heeded me not; the moment the

LORD thy God's back is turned, the pair of you are at it, yea, even like knives.

25 And Adam spake unto God, saying: all work and no play, et cetera et cetera, I trust I do not have to draw pictures, you are a God of the world.

26 And the LORD God said, Behold, the man thinks he is become yet mightier than one of us, to have a lie in *on the* seventh day and not do a hand's turn, and let the business that I have given unto him go unto pot; it will be golf next.

27 Therefore the LORD God sent him forth from the garden centre and home-mart of Eden, and caused a notice *to be* put in the window, saying: closed for alterations.

28 So he drove out the man; and he placed at the east of Eden Cherubim, *and a* flaming sword which turned every way; and he caused to be brought in the six-day week for a punishment and a sign, until such time as the earth was ready to receive his saints.

Negative Vetting

Prince Andrew and Miss Ferguson are on common ground in that neither has played, nor is ever likely to play, polo.

The Times

'SAY WHAT you like about royalty,' said the man in the herringbone overcoat, forefingering crisp crumbs from the marblette table-top with practised stabs, 'when it comes to marriage, they leave nothing to chance.'

'They've probably got a whole department,' said the man in the QPR scarf. He drained his lager, and on a soft eructative descant, added, 'or a computer.'

'Bound to,' said the small man. 'It does not bear thinking about, having to put your finger on a non-polo-playing fiancée by manual means. Could take years.'

'In *those* circles,' emphasized the man in the herringbone overcoat.

'Naturally in *those* circles,' snapped the small man irritably. 'I do not, I trust, have to dot every sodding T. If I was not talking about *those* circles it would have been a different story, if it was *me* looking for a suitable life's companion, coming up with one who didn't like polo would be a doddle. One who didn't like Tupperware, on the other hand, could be tricky.'

'They would have to watch theirselves, mind, doing it with a wossname, computer,' said the man in the QPR scarf. 'I read in the paper where she drove a Volkswagen Golf and didn't like polo. Ask a computer to find one like that and it could very easily come up with one who drove a Volkswagen

Polo and didn't like golf. I speak as one who has been known to receive a gas bill for the man up the road.'

The man in the herringbone overcoat nodded.

'It is on the cards,' he said, 'that he would not find out till he came down of a morning carrying a bag of clubs and spotted her sat in a crash helmet at the far end of the table having a go at her boiled egg with a mallet. It could very well end up with him giving the Archbishop a bell and asking him to come round sharpish with his annulment kit.'

The small man considered this for a time.

'She would not hit an egg with a mallet,' he said, 'even if she did like polo. They do not carry on like that in those circles.'

'Wrong!' cried the man in the herringbone overcoat. 'That is *exactly* how they carry on in those circles. They are always bunging food about. Some of these catered functions, you cannot see a hand in front of your face for flying bread-rolls et cetera. It is my guess that if you asked a computer for one who didn't like chucking dinner about, it would come up with sod all.'

'It is an interesting approach,' said the man in the QPR scarf, reflectively, 'going out looking for one who *doesn't* like sunnink. Most people I know look for ones who do like sunnink.'

'Such as?' enquired the man in the herringbone overcoat.

'Such as,' said the man in the QPR scarf, 'artificial playing surfaces.'

The other two looked at him, over their rims.

'Is that why you never married?' enquired the man in the herringbone overcoat. 'On account of being unable to find one who liked astroturf?'

'It is easy,' said the man in the QPR scarf, 'to see you have never tried taking one to a home fixture. It starts asking silly bloody questions about why they fall over and do not get muddy etcetera, you do not know where to look. You could not spend your life with a woman like that. What would you talk about?'

'There we are, then,' said the small man. 'It only proves my point. If you had a computer, you could probably press a button and eliminate all those who didn't like astroturf. I do not pretend to be an expert in these matters, but I have been about a bit and it is my impression that if they can put a man on the moon, they ought to be able to weed out fiancées who prefer grass.'

'That, after all,' said the man in the herringbone overcoat, nodding, 'is the way the Palace has gone about it. It is a very sensible approach to marriage, in my view. Imagine if he *had* ended up with one who liked polo, due to computer error, and Runcie had refused to let him jack it in on account of bringing the church into disrepute and him possibly ending up as the Archbishop of the Canterbury Bingo Hall. What kind of marriage would that be?'

'Come home of an evening,' said the small man, 'no hot dinner, note under the clock, *Off Up The Polo, I Think There Was Some Cold Pork Somewhere.*'

'It does not bear thinking about,' said the man in the herringbone overcoat. 'Fourth in line and you come back to a dark house, nothing on the telly, she probably hasn't even recorded *Crown Court.*'

'He would very likely stick one on her when she got in,' said the small man. 'I had an uncle in the Fleet Air Arm, his old woman was never out of plaster.'

'I take your point,' said the man in the QPR scarf, albeit somewhat grudgingly. He went off to the bar, and came back with three fresh pints. 'I wonder if they both don't like thin glasses,' he said.

'We may never know,' said the man in the herringbone overcoat. 'I can't see it as a major problem, mind.'

'You can never be sure,' said the man in the QPR scarf. 'Personally, I think there is nothing less feminine than a woman drinking out of a jug. How do we know he does not feel the same? It could well be they forgot to put that one in the computer, they could be up some banquet somewhere, she would say, *Can I have it in a tankard?*, there'd be a geezer there from the *Sun* disguised as a pig's head with an apple in its gob, rest of him under the table taking shorthand, I trust I do not have to draw pictures?'

'IT'S BIG JUGS WEEK IN THE SUN!' offered the small man.

'No question,' said the man in the QPR scarf.

The man in the herringbone overcoat whittled a pork scratching to a sliver and reamed his ear with it, ruminatively.

'It has to be bloody big computer,' he said at last. 'You can see where her five million goes. It would not surprise me if all that is left of Buckingham Palace is the facade. Climb through a window and you would find nothing but a lot of keyboards and little green screens and blokes in white overalls walking about.'

'It is probably like sunnink out of Bond,' said the man in the QPR scarf, 'where they walk into a volcano and it all looks like a big branch of Dixons.'

'It could well explain,' said the small man, 'why they let Michael Fagan off.'

'To shut his mouth,' said the man in the herringbone overcoat, nodding. 'Good point.'

'He never sat on her bed at all,' said the small man. 'I always reckoned that sounded a bit iffy. It is very likely she never sets foot in the place, she probably has a small flat in Maida Vale, it is probably all she can afford after shelling out her Civil List on a giant computer, they probably keep one room back for investitures and the odd fork supper for visiting blackies, the rest is all wires and microchips.'

'It would have to be,' said the man in the herringbone overcoat, firmly. 'How many women are there in the world?'

'Two thousand million,' said the small man.

'And how many things are there for 'em not to like?'

'Including astroturf?' enquired the man in the QPR scarf. 'Could be billions. Cats, lightning, giblets, doing your toenails in the kitchen, you name it.'

'And once you'd put all *that* in,' said the man in the herringbone overcoat, jabbing his finger towards his companions, 'you would have to run it all off against the things *he* didn't like, including things he didn't know he didn't like yet because he didn't know there was anything not to like, e.g. where some of 'em are funny about you smelling your socks to see if there's another day in 'em –'

'That is a closed book to the single man.'

'– with all that, it is amazing they ever find anybody.'

'No,' said the man in the QPR scarf, 'what is really incredible, statistically speaking, is that, when you consider that one woman in four is Chinese, the computer didn't find him a yellow one.'

'They probably all play polo,' said the small man.

Closely Observed Strains

JUST SHOWS you.

I had always imagined librarianship to be as stressful a calling as you could shake a stethoscope at.

Examine the average librarian's molars, I believed, and you would find them ground down to gum level. Strap that puny sun-starved upper arm to a sphygmomanometer, I thought, and the blood-pressure would rocket to the top of the dial, ring a bell, and drop a coconut in your lap. Glance through the bars of your neighbourhood madhouse, I was convinced, and you would be confronted with the heart-rending spectacle of shrieking bibliophobes bouncing from wall to wall like squashballs.

These assumptions were not speculative. They were – rare for me – all inferred from actual observation. I have never stood in line at my own local branch without finding myself behind a string of irascible old biddies in big white shoes slagging off the harassed stamper for everything from the non-arrival of an ordered truckload of Barbara Cartland to the fact that pp 76-77 of *First Among Equals* contained a flat wasp. Not a visit has passed without an elderly cove in a seersucker suit threatening to drag the librarian off his stool and brolly him within a inch of his life for daring to levy a fine on a book taken out on VJ-Day but understandably misplaced during the subsequent street party and thus honestly believed lost. Nor can I count the occasions upon which decent Jekylls have, before my eyes, turned into savage Hydes at the polite suggestion that they return home and get their ticket before attempting to carry off the library's property.

Since an average day will see this punctuated with the din of either a child being crushed by a dislodged shelfload of *Sam Pig*, a mature foreign student shrieking about his civil rights when spotted stuffing technical magazines in his bonk-bag, or an old drunk reminding everyone within a two-mile radius of his war record upon being evicted for snoring in the reference section, I had quite reasonably imagined librarians to be a race more prone than most to tic and infarct.

I have never been more wrong. Nothing, it transpires, could be further from the truth, and for this I find myself indebted, albeit obliquely, to Mr Arthur Scargill. For at last week's NUM Conference, Mr Scargill stood up and waved a report compiled by Manchester University in which 58 professions were listed in order of stressfulness. Mr Scargill, of course, did not wave this report in order to bring me to my senses on the question of librarians; he waved it in order to prove that mining was the most stressful job of all, that being the finding of Manchester University. Mining topped the list.

Now, while most of you will have been wondering why Mr Scargill should choose to draw attention to this grim fact when he is clearly the main reason why miners have been breaking out in hives and gnawing the skirting-board – a theory quickly endorsed by the fact that the second most stressful occupation is policeman – I found my own heart clattering to a somewhat different note.

For, once we remove miners and policemen from the list on self-explanatory grounds, what are we left with? We are left with journalists at the top, and librarians at the bottom. While the journalist screams, sweats, gasps and palpitates towards his premature box, the librarian glides serenely through his job-extended life with so little to tense his tissue that all an embalmer is required to do when the librarian decides to call it a day at 105 is slightly straighten the smile on the departed's face to reduce unseemly glee.

I cannot begin to guess why this should be so. Manchester University does not expatiate. It just makes lists. Nor do I particularly wish to *know* why it should be so. I wish only that the list had been available thirty years ago. The careers master was, for a bleak misanthrope, relatively enthusiastic about journalism. Travel, glamour, influence, expenses, name in the paper, all that. Another Hannan Swaffer. Another Nat Buggins. Gubbins, sir. Are you contradicting me, boy?

Nothing about blood vessels popping like Tizer bubbles; nothing about arteries snapping like pipe-stems.

And yet, and yet. Need it be, even now, too late?

Coincidence is a strange fruit. Ask any greengrocer. The day upon which Arthur Scargill chose to wave his seminal pamphlet just happened to be the selfsame day upon which two other items of possibly incalculable import collided.

The first was yet another list, this time cobbled together by the Faculty of Community Medicine at the Royal College of Physicians. It was published in the *Daily Telegraph*.

It was a list of bad places to be if you were 48.

The worst place to be is Britain. It is the unhealthiest place in the world. Particularly for those prone to the effects of stress, because its death rate from heart disease is higher than anywhere else's. If you are 48 in Britain, your life expectancy is a further 25 years. If you are 48 in France, your life expectancy is a further 26 years, in Norway it is 27 years, in Greece it is 29.

But in Iceland, top of the list, it is a corking 30.

Care to guess the third coincidence of that day?

My birthday.

Care to guess which?

I have, of course, been laying down certain plans for the mid-life crisis for some time. You cannot be caught on the hop when the mortal coil takes a seasonal lurch. Such best-laid schemes as I have hitherto laid, however, were drawn up before the NUM Conference, and thus concerned them-selves with activities I need no longer specify, since – in the light of what we now know – they would in all probability lead to a black line being drawn at the bottom of life's spotty ledger before I had even got my left sock off.

And what is it that we now know?

We know that for a 48-year-old British hack, there can be only one option.

Shall I enjoy it in rural Stykkishólmur, I wonder? A white clapboard Pørtakabin overlooking the ice-pocked fjørd, a mute gull standing on the hand-lettered BØKS sign above the corrugated-iron door, an elderly spinster assistant in grey lisle stockings and elastoplasted bifocals scuttling furtively behind the serried Dexion lest I catch her eye and, too long in celibate exile, forget the hypertensive risks; a flaking oil-stove, a rubber-plant, one red ink-pad and one black, a green steel cabinet of indexed titles, and one smeared window, treble-glazed against the Arctic breeze, through which I watch my little file of clients, plum-tinted by the Northern Lights, plodding on showshoes up the frozen hill.

'Gød mørning, Agnes Agnesdottir!'

'Gød mørning, Coren Corensson!'

'Snø again, ik see!'

'And mør snø expekted!'

'Støne mi! Did yø enjøy *Die Prødigal Dottir*?'

'Ø ja! Hev yø die niuew øne?'

'Et ist øn ørder, Agnes Agnesdottir. Yø fuled in der førm?'

'Øf cørse. Und her ar die bøks ik børøed lars wik.'

'Denke. Ø wøt ist dis? Strøbirry yam?'

'Nø, Coren Corensson, ik hed a nøseblid.'

'Pul dis øne, Agnes Agnesdottir! Dis hes gøt a pip øn it!'

'Dø nøt get engry, remember yør blød-pressur!'

'Hø richt yø ar, Agnes Agnesdottir! Gød tag!'

'Gød tag, Coren Corensson!'

Just think – can it really be only a couple of short days ago that I was planning to eat, drink, smoke, wench, scribble, and stress my way into an early grave at 73?

Crazy? I'll say I was crazy!

You get to 48, and it takes Arthur Scargill to tell you what life's all about.

Heir Conditioning

On February 27, the fiftieth anniversary of his death, a special ceremony at the Russian Academy of Sciences will be held to honour the life and work of Ivan Petrovich Pavlov.

The Times

IN THE spring of 19——, in the neglected garden of an elegant if somewhat ramshackle house at the corner of N—— Street in the ——ern suburbs of the town of P——, a small black dog was to be discovered deep in earnest conversation with a large ginger cat.

'I find myself in an extremely embarrassing situation, esteemed Tiddles Tiddlesova,' began the dog, after the normal courtesies had been observed.

'Do not think, respected Fido Fidoyevich,' replied the cat, 'that you are alone in your discomfort. Under the obligations placed upon us by the conventions of normal social behaviour, I should by now have had one of your eyes out.'

'And I, in my turn,' said the dog, nodding gravely, 'should have bitten an ear off, at the very least. However, these are, you will agree, by no means normal times. That is why I have taken the liberty of addressing you personally, in the hope that we may together resolve the unsettling situation with which we would appear to be confronted.'

The cat looked at him. Behind her collar, an atavistic hackle, willy-nilly, rose.

'I take leave, Fido Fidoyevich, to regard the word *unsettling* as something of an understatement,' she said, coldly. 'Last night, as I advanced upon a saucered pilchard, I received a most dreadful shock.'

The dog shuddered.

'How I sympathize, dear Tiddles Tiddlesova!' he exclaimed. 'Can there be anything more horrifying in the middle of the night than to come upon something lying in a congealed pool of tomato sauce with its head off?'

At this, the feline hackle rose yet further, disturbing as it did so her collar, from which hung a little silver bell.

The bell tinkled.

The dog began to dribble.

The cat, though she could not prevent herself from glowering at him with more than usual distaste, allowed, of course, good manners to prevail, and merely said, albeit tightly:

'You do not *quite* understand, Fido Fidoyevich. The shock I refer to was entirely real. My fur stood on end. My teeth twanged. My diddly twitched. The lights dimmed.'

The dog's already wrinkled brow yet further furrowed.

'It does, so I have heard, happen with eels,' he murmured. 'But an electric *pilchard*?'

'The blame lay not with the fish,' snapped Tiddles Tiddlesova, 'but with our deranged master Ivan Petrovich Pavlov! He, I am convinced, is at the bottom of it. As the lights flickered, I could not but observe his shadowy figure in a corner of the scullery, scribbling feverishly in a large red notebook.'

'I know the very book!' cried Fido Fidoyevich.

'I had not finished!' shrilled his companion furiously, with such penetrating pitch that a window next door, at Number ——b, was flung open, allowing a large riding boot to be hurled into the Pavlov garden, where it struck a dustbin, displacing its lid. At the reverberant clang, the toolshed door opened. A chimpanzee emerged, turned a deft somersault, pressed a lever, removed from its little tray a walnut thus released, went back inside, and carefully closed the door behind it.

'Forgive me,' murmured Fido Fidoyevich, when all was still again, 'do go on, dear Tiddles Tiddlesova. What happened next?'

'I was, of course, still hungry. I therefore approached the fish again, but more circumspectly.'

'To any avail?'

'To no avail. I merely received two more frightful electric shocks. Clearly, there is some manner of short circuit somewhere, which our distracted master is presently too preoccupied to repair. One does not understand such mundane mechanical things, nor wish to. It is not for those of breeding. What is far more significant is the fact that each time, upon my receiving the shock, Ivan Petrovich Pavlov immediately began scribbling.'

The dog pursed his still salivating lips in puzzlement, and licked the emergent blob as genteelly, all things considered, as he could.

'Most curious,' he muttered. 'It would appear that every time you received a shock, it triggered some strange response in our master which set him writing. It does, of course, fit in utterly with my own observations concerning his continuingly neurotic behaviour. Here, too, food seems to be of the essence. Every day, just before my lunch, he has taken to ringing a hand-bell. Immediately thereafter – I have considered it prudent to keep one eye upon him while eating – the same scribbling follows. Does, perhaps, the sight of animals –'

'Domestic pets.'

'– domestic pets at lunch inspire him to some creative activity? An ode? A charcoal portrait? Or is it that some deep, forgive me, sexual–'

'You don't half go on,' said a voice.

'I beg your pardon?' said the dog. 'Did you say something, Tiddles Tiddlesova?'

The ginger cat shifted uneasily.

'Forgive me, Fido Fidoyevich,' she murmured awkwardly. 'It was not I that spoke. I have, I am afraid, a flea.'

'Pray do not be concerned, dear Tiddles Tiddlesova,' countered the dog quickly, 'it will go no further.'

'Shows how much you know about fleas,' said the voice.

The gallant Fido Fidoyevich ignored it.

'There is need for neither embarrassment nor apology,' he assured the cat, warmly. 'The common flea, if you will permit me a small though not I think infelicitous pleasantry, is our common bane.'

'*Hay small though not High think infelicitous pleasantry,*' mocked the voice, from somewhere on the cat's left flank. 'You want to watch who you're calling common, tovarich. In fact, as a lickspittle – in your case literally – lackey of the infamous bourgeoisie, you would be well advised to guard your gob generally.'

'Oh, really?'

'*Ho really!*' replied the voice, this time from the cat's foreleg. 'May I remind you that this is 19——? Mother Russia stands poised on the brink of a great, a mighty surging tide is, nothing can resist a wossname whose time has, it's all in the books, ask anybody. The flea's flag is deepest red, etcetera.'

'I believe there is a collar one can buy,' murmured Fido Fidoyevich solicitously, into his companion's ginger ear.

'I am touched by your concern, dear Fido Fidoyevich,' replied Tiddles Tiddlesova, 'but I fear that our master's present derangement precludes his attention to such—'

'Derangement?' cried the flea, from her rump. 'I shall note that down! I shall place that upon record! I shall raise that at the next plenary session! Come the Revolution, you will very likely end up as a muff. Comrade Pavlov is an inspiration to us all. Without him, us fleas would not know one end of a wheelbarrow from another. We would still be under the Tsarist thumb, or, more accurately thumbnail, i.e. splat! We would not be able to play a role in the exhilarating days that lie ahead.'

'Wheelbarrow?' enquired the ginger cat faintly, of her left hindquarter. 'Not,' she added, 'that I normally talk to parasites.'

'Look who is calling who parasite!' shrieked the flea. 'Bloody lie around all day, nice fire, monogrammed bleeding porringer, fresh milk, own flap, waited on hand and foot, never lift a finger. You ought to try it out there in the cold, foraging for a living, dodging the Flit and the rolled-up newspaper, trying to find a bit of scab or dandruff to bring home to the family. *Who are the parasites now?*'

'What do you mean wheelbarrow?' persisted Tiddles Tiddlesova.

Reverence calmed the flea.

'Our great leader,' it said softly, 'has harnessed the power of the workers. You would not credit what he's got in the loft. Five thousand fleas, titchy wheelbarrows, titchy cranes, titchy treadmills, you would not credit the industrial organization, every time he rings his bell we are at it hammer and wossname. End of the day, everybody sits down to a nice blood supper. From each according to his abilities,' incanted the worker, its voice trembling as only a flea's can, 'to each according to his needs.'

Tiddles Tiddlesova, in the heavy silence that followed, turned slowly to the dog.

'All I get for supper,' she said, 'is electric shocks.'

'*Il faut épater les bourgeois*,' said the flea, smugly. 'Our great leader is showing the oppressors the new dawn. They will work for their dinner. They will come when they are called, they will say please, comrade, and thank you, comrade. Henceforth, it is not us fleas that will hop about. If you do not like it, the line forms over here for the 20,000 volts, catch my drift?'

Fido Fidoyevich shook his head.

'This is all beyond me,' he murmured. 'What is going on? Where will it end?'

And, in coincident answer, a distant yet a penetrating bell began rhythmically to clang. The dog, of course, merely salivated; but, a mile away, as the train drew slowly into the station, Lenin upon the cowcatcher and the bell pealing above his head, a hundred thousand caps, as if upon a reflex, were hurled into the air.

A Statement from the Board of British Humour

Dear Consumer:

Until quite recently, it was universally acknowledged that British Humour plc (formerly the British Joke Corporation) led the field in the manufacture of high quality products which, both at home and throughout the world, made people fall down and roll about.

Wherever one looked in the marketing spectrum – from comic novels concerning soppy aunts to funny walks performed by men with risible toupees, from boarding house farces involving rarely fewer than eight amusing adulterers to jocular songs about prostate disorder, from major Egyptian sand dances to the widest variety of things poured down the front of trousers the world had ever seen – British Humour plc was a byword for comic quality at competitive prices, no job too large or small.

Even today, all over the globe, many a solid hand-built BH item is still in regular service, still utterly reliable, still giving complete satisfaction to the fortunate consumer. Ten thousand miles from the Glasgow Empire, a heathen Chinee will suddenly collapse chortling in his paddy field at the memory of a chicken crossing a road, a plucky Gurkha will clutch his ribs at the recollection of a particularly ingenious squint, the high-pitched shriek of a lonely Eskimo will echo across the barren ice-floes as its owner recalls for the thousandth time – though every bit as fresh as the day it first trundled off the assembly line – what the bishop said to the actress.

All this, however, is no longer enough. The humour industry has rolled on apace, transglobal agglomerates have entered the field, new mass markets have been generated and demand new mass products. It is therefore no longer possible for us at British Humour to fill our foreign order books simply by constructing a single, stoutly built, lovingly crafted, hand-polished one about the deaf midget and the three-legged barmaid.

By the same token, time and fashion have not dealt kindly with many of our most cherished marques. The Sambo, the Ikey Mo, the Big Bum, the Mother-in-Law, the Funny Smell In Here, the What's Worn Under The Kilt, the Take My Wife, have all proved impossible to adapt to contemporary demands, although one or two, of course, are still produced in small local workshops for individual clients like Mr Bernard Manning; while, in the cartoon field, the Desert Island, the Bed Of Nails, the Pearly Gate, the Psychiatrist's Couch, and many more trusty old favourites are now on their last knockings; and as for the comic novel, the only model still in regular production – the one about an English academic going to a loony foreign conference – can only be purchased (or indeed manufactured) secondhand.

It was thus inevitable that the Executive Board of British Humour should have decided on the brilliantly enterprising plan of selling the good bits to the highest international bidder. Not surprisingly, there has been something of a public outcry, and patriots throughout the realm have expressed horror at the thought of a Belgian Funny Walk, a Slovak adaptation of *Charley's Aunt*, a Burmese impression of Tommy Cooper, two Algerians singing *Underneath the Arches*, of any Canadian doing anything at all; but we at British Humour plc feel this to be naught but a knee-jerk reaction based, albeit understandably, on a combination of nostalgia and nationalism. The plain truth is that our national comic production is doomed unless it globalizes, but that the adaptation to the new demands need not be as black as it has been painted. Let me offer you a few telling examples.

REDNOSE-PRATFALL

In recent years, while Rednose-Pratfall, the Wigan-based producer of low-budget family knockabouts for the domestic market, has just about managed to keep its head above water by refurbishing old models for such fleet operators as Cannon & Ball, Little & Large, and so on, it has become clear to most analysts that the writing is on the wall; where, indeed, much of it appears to have been done.

Simply by adding a bit of smutty trim here, or a go-fast catch-phrase there, one merely staves off the evil day when recognition comes that a joke has no more mileage in it. When, therefore, the mighty General Boffola Corporation of America came to us and explained that their Wacky Sitcom Division was in urgent need of models capable of conversion to the Stateside market, we eagerly accepted their offer to take over Rednose-Pratfall *in toto*.

Now, before the patriots among you rush to your placards and MPs, let me just say one thing: *this is no sellout of our precious heritage*. On the contrary, this will in fact mean a new lease of life for many old British favourites such as Take My Wife, I Won't Say She's Fat, But, which, without losing its basic identity, will not only become more caring, more feminist, and – I believe the word is – zany, it will also turn into a twenty-six-part series designed to cash in on the enormous Plump Liberation market.

There's just no way that we at British Humour plc could do that.

TAKE THE NIPS

For some years now, we at British Humour have struggled in vain to penetrate the lucrative Japanese market.

It is extremely difficult with the resources at our disposal to export comedy to the Japs, who fall all over the place at the sight of excruciating pain, but little else. To take an obvious instance, a typically British joke built for the domestic user and concerning a man going into a chemist's shop would stand no chance at all in the Nipponese market unless the man ended up – probably as the result of a misconstrued monosyllabic shout – receiving a bamboo enema while simultaneously having his nose bitten off by the pharmacist's dog.

How, then, you will ask, can we earn valuable hard foreign currency through the export of our comic expertise to Japan without compromising our reputation?

Quite simply, is my answer. As the result of a far-sighted bilateral deal between our There Was This Bloke Division and the All Bones Break Right Now Corporation of Kyoto, jokes designed by All Bones Break Right Now will be shipped to Bradford as components and assembled by British craftsmen at the old Bradford Alhambra works.

Of course, we have had to guarantee that at least 20% of the finished material will be for British consumption, and it may thus be necessary, for example, for *So, Minister!* to include a weekly scene in which a senior Cabinet adviser ritually disembowels himself, or for *The Two Lonnies* to decapitate one another from time to time, but this is, surely, a small price to pay for the remunerative export to Japan of the bulk of the comedy thus manufactured.

THE PARBLEU-GORBLIMEY PROJECT

For more than a century, humorists on both sides of the Channel have dreamed of forming an Anglo-French comic consortium with the object of selling cheap mass-produced yuks that would sell equally well in England and France.

Not surprisingly, this has invariably met with uninformed and bigoted resistance by the two populations. The British feared that their traditional security could be violated by a flood of ooh-la-la cuckoldry jokes striking at the very heart of British marital confidence, endless recitals by satirical petomaniacs playing flatulent renditions of *Land of Hope and Glory* on their undraped orifices, and, worst of all, mime; while the French were terrified of, quite simply, everything British, from the total incomprehensibility of P.G. Wodehouse to being hit in the face by a custard pie not made from true *crème patissière*.

The agreement, at last, upon the Fixed Link joke has changed all that at a stroke. It will now be possible, by a technique jointly developed by British Humour plc and Drôlerie Française SA, to make the smooth transition from an English joke to a French one by way of a Franglais link – for example:

... replied: 'But it's not as big as the gasman's! *Not as big as the gasman's!* Where *do* I get 'em from! And maintenant, un song, un petit song, entitled Elle Etait Only Un Cobbler's Daughter, Mais Elle Couldn't Half Make It Last! Musique, maestro, s'il vous plaît!'

At which point, of course, a French comedian would come on and sing something in his own incomprehensible language.

THE GUINNESS BID

Finally, I must reply to all those of you anxious about the recent Guinness offer for 51% of the shares in Sure And Begob, the ailing British Humour plc subsidiary recently hived off in the hope not only of widening share ownership, in line with Government policy, but also of helping bring both sides of the Border together, in line with the Anglo-Irish Agreement.

It was believed at the time that there was enormous potential left in the Irish joke, which could be realized by an injection of fresh capital. Since the flotation last June, however, only one new model has been produced:

A man was sitting in a Kerry pub, when the door opened, and another man came in.
'Is it still raining outside,' enquired the first man, 'begob?'

'Sure and bejabers,' replied the second man, 'and how would I know? I'm a stranger here meself.'

Unfortunately, when the model was unveiled at the February board meeting, uproar broke out. Provisional Shareholders fought hand-to-hand with members of King Billy's Own Loyal Debenture 9% on every imaginable aspect of the product – should the pub be in Kerry or Derry, should it be raining or snowing or just a bit windy, which man was the Catholic and which the Protestant, did the door open inwards or outwards, could you get a bit of hot food, was there a dart-board, did they have one of them piles of pennies the Catholics/Protestants was always nicking for the ould meter, and so forth.

The meeting having ended with the arrival of troops from both sides of the Border and the collapse of the shares, a bid was immediately entered by Guinness, who – as I understand it – plan to rebuild the joke at Park Royal as:

A man was sitting in a pub, when the door opened, and another man came in.

'Is it still raining outside,' enquired the first man, 'begob?'

'Sure and bejabers,' replied the second man, 'and how would I know? I'm drinking Guinness, the world's finest stout.'

Nothing lost there, I feel sure you'll agree. And, I feel equally certain, all the assurance you could want that here at British Humour plc, we shall continue to move ever onward and upward into the broad sunny uplands, making our place in the annals of international comedy stronger than ever.

Of course, it may not look very much at present, but,

together, we can make it grow into something very substantial indeed. As, so I have been given to understand, the bishop said to the actress.

Chief Executive,
Silly Articles Division

So Goodbye, Dear, and Amen

According to expert astronomical opinion, Halley's Comet could be anything from a billion-ton snowball to an insubstantial exhalation hardly larger than the average Tesco. Whatever it was, it has been coming and going every seventy-six years, and, as these authentic gobbets show, never once failed to disappoint us.

JANUARY 1606

Fawkes goinge on with much plainte, his thummes havynge been bente bak by the patent digitorquendo™ newlie imported from Spayne and the bukkit not yet emptyed these fyve weakes, but despyte the hammerynge of the scafolde, the poor sole lives in hoap. Hee has yet another of his foolprufe planns, wich is that, as he ascendes to the blok, the blazing lite of the Commit will so stryke the upswung blaid as to dazzel the gards, executioner, assembled gildsmen and so forthe. Fawkes wil then spryng from the stepps, nok a mounted halbàrdier from his charger with one mity blo, and, vaultyng the gait, be at Wopping before his persecuters have recover'd their site, where hee wil take shippe for Antwerp disgised as a butte of porter.

Hee is so much cheared by this new plotte that I do not have it in my harte to disabuse him of its chaunces. Yesternyte, I stood upon Thos. Bates's sholdres and peer'd through our litle slotte, attemptynge to locate the Commit from a sketch of the Hev'ns in the *London Gazette*. If I have it aright, it is the size of a warte, and wuld not dazle a flye.

OCTOBER 1066

*Deux ou troyes minutes apres le daybarquement, nous
avons trouvay l'armay du Roy Harold en pleyn air dans une
situation vrayment incroyable!*
   *Ni les soldats ni les chevaliers nous fayent aucune
attention!*
   *Tous le monde amblayent vaguement sur le plage, les
casques sous les bras, les yeues au ciel, en cryant:*
'Stone me, is that it, over there?'
et
'What sort of tail are we after, is it a furry effort, or what?'
et
'Hang about, I think Eggnog's spotted sunnink!'
et
'Look up there, your Majesty, near that gull, or am I wrong?'
   *Immediatement, nous avons tiray les arcs, et le Roy est
tombay comme une brique, la fleche en oeil. Plus de rosbif et
des pommes rotis et le pounding rolipoli pour lui!
Vrayment,c'est une race bizarre.*

AUGUST 1378

A thynne and sallowe man was thir bisyde,
To bee to us our astronomicke guide;
For al men knowe thatte committs in hir courses,
Whilom they fryghte the dogges and bolte the horses,
Affeckte *us* straungely; thus, to eese our feere,
Astronomers buy cheepe and eke sel deere,
Havynge aboute them boans and chartes and swich
Wherein they reed the runes – and reep the riche
Rewardes thatte Chryste Hymselfe confyrmes awayte
Thatte man who passes inne through Heven's gayte:
Tho whether passynge inne while stil on Erthe –
And takynge Heven's boones to swel one's girthe
Bye sellynge off the stuf that one has lerned
To those less blessed – is not to bee spern'd,

I knowe not. Lette us not proceede from spyte,
(For aught I woot, he was a worthie wight)
And simplie telle how we wayfaring soules,
Bewitch'd by tales of white dwarfes and blacke holes,
And (tremblynge in the inkye Kentish darke),
A yarne yclept the Huntynge of the Quark,
Fel utterlie beneeth this felwe's spell.
And whenne, as dawne broake o'er thatte dewie dell,
He cross't hymself and warned us of the Committ,
We al beganne to shreeke (and some to vomit).
But 'Feere not, frends!' hee cryed. 'For, tho it comes,
Salvatioun canne be yores for quyte smal sums!
See, I have mermayde's boans and werewolf's feet,
And swich fyne antidoats, to more than meete
Yore needes whenne thysse abominacioun visits!'
Wee culd not waite to purchase these requisits.
Hee solde oute quyte. Then murmured, 'I must goe
To gette more stock from thysse bloak that I knowe.'
We watched hys horse cross the horizonne's rim:
Wee never saw the Committ; nay, nor him.

SEPTEMBER 1758

Upon my commenting upon the rapid deterioration of his new catchpenny headgear and the evidence it offered of its imminent passage into not desuetude alone but also derisibility, he rejoindered: 'Sir, when a man is tired of wearing a hat testifying to his having seen Halley's Comet, he is tired of life. That nor I, nor no-one else, has in fact set one eye upon the thing is neither here nor there. As to the Astronomer Royal, however, I would say only that if he continues to draw his sinecure on the grounds that the nocturnal welkin is entertaining a distinguished visitor, why, Sir, when he leaves our houses let us count our spoons.'

I was so bemused by this that I left the good Doctor forthwith and, finding myself unaccountably upon the towpath beneath Blackfriars Bridge and in the presence of a fetching young mulatto who enquired as to whether I should care to spend a groat to see her little comet, as she put it, I instantly took advantage of her admirable topical enterprise. Upon my polite enquiry as to my performance, however, imagine my chagrin when the wanton replied: 'Like a dog's walking on his hinder legs, it was not done well, but I was surprised to find it done at all.'

Sgr. Andrea Pisano,
Gli Laburni,
Firenze.   MARCH 1302

Caro Pisano,
Wossa goin on widda dissa crackapot? Woddi takea me for? He'sa you lousy fren, you innatroducin him, you tella me wossa up.

I gotta de innavoice inna frun of me as I write. Issa for one best quality Adoration Of De Magi, sixa by four, top oil finish, nice frame, string, two hooks. Now you a professional, wossa your idea of an Adoration? Issa got one oly family, one angel, three kings, coupla shepherds, one ox, one donnerkey, plus shed, right? Up above, issa gotta star.

Issa notta gotta cometo.

I show you fren de finish pitcher, I tella him I chuckin in two coats varnish bukshee.

Wotti say?

'Grazie, Maestro Giotto di Bondone'?

'Issa bloody knockout, Maestro Giotto di Bondone'?

'Iss gonna look ace inna my den, Maestro Giotto di Bondone'?

No.

You fren say: 'Issa notta gotta cometo.'

I say: 'Wot?'

You fren say: 'Issa cometo inna de sky. Everybody talkin about it. Everybody gettin pitchers painted. Issa alla de rage.'

I say: 'Lissen, fartaface, you order a Adoration, you get a Adoration, you no getta cometo, wotta kine cowboy operation you think we runnin here?'

You fren say: 'No cometto, no lire.'

I no smacka him inna de gob. Dissa notta my way. I walka to de winnadow, I open, I say: 'Show me dissa cometto, dickahead!'

You fren say: 'Maybe issa roun de back. Anyway, wossa matter witchew, you a artisto, wotchew needa to see a cometto for, you make one up.'

Tella me, Pisano, wotta should I do? I enclose a sketch. Should I commapromise my artissertic innategrity? Issa dis too commercial?

Justa one cometto?

Vostro devotissimo,
Giotto

Their Blue Heaven

Shrugging off media hysteria about Prince Andrew's imminent nuptials, the Duke of Edinburgh observed: 'I don't know what all the fuss is about, it's just a marriage like any other.'

Daily Telegraph

Dear Mr Coren:
I am very interested in Royal precedent, e.g. going into a revolving door and who sits next to the piccalilli etcetera, and what I should like to know is if they decided to go to a film only they both had other things on first e.g. chiropodist, trooping a colour, having the cat seen to, and they had to meet outside the Odeon, would she have to hang about never mind him being late, or would she buy the tickets with her own money and wait inside, or would she go in and save the seat next to her and tell the usherette to show him where she was sitting when he turned up?
Rhoda Vansittart, Tring

Generally speaking, this situation is fully covered by the Consort Entitlement Statute of 1485, when, following the Battle of Bosworth, Anne, wife to Richard III, was allowed by the Lord Chancellor to start dinner without her husband on the grounds that his head was on a stick in the next county. Since then, Royal spouses have as a rule been

79

permitted to depart from due precedent according to strict and clearly delineated example.

It is doubtful whether standing outside the Odeon falls within the given categories. Usually, the Master of the Local Paper will have informed the Royal couple in writing as to the exact time of the film's beginning, since they will have made known to him well in advance their gracious desire not to sit through all the adverts and other rubbish, and a Moving Picture Equerry (or, in Scotland, a Fleapit Ensign of the Queen's Troop) will have been charged with ensuring that both Royal personages arrive at the box-office simultaneously, where a Ticket-Major of the Household Cavalry will be waiting with two best stalls.

Should, however, such arrangements go uncharacteristically awry and the consort arrive first, she should on no account wait outside. She should present herself to the Manager, who will then implement the Purple Emergency Procedures kept in all cinemas for this contingency, which involve a child, a bouquet, an inspection of the commissionaire, and a complimentary box of Maltesers.

Dear Mr Coren:
Could you tell me which of them will do the milk order of an evening and do they have one of those titchy crate efforts or do they just sort of put the empty bottles on the step? Also, will the one who does it also take the bins out?
M. Hastings, Rhyl

With the exception of HM The Queen, whose empties are put out nightly by Bottle Pursuivant, members of the Royal Family traditionally take it in turns to write the note to their milkman, except in cases of grave illiteracy. Clearly, it would not do for messages such as *2 pintes Gole Top, 6 egs, and have them rarsbry yogerts come in yet if so leeve 3 and oblig* to fall into the wrong hands.

Yes, they do have a small crate, no different from yours and mine except that it is made of tit-proof gold, affixed to the doorscraper by the Chain of Scone, and guarded by a platoon of Gurkhas. As for the bins, these are not handled personally by any member of the Royal Family but carried out each night by the Gentleman Usher of the Black Bag.

Dear Mr Coren:
At Tesco's, would protocol require him to wait in the car reading the _Greyhound Express_, claiming there were meter people all over, and leaving her to lug the boxes out herself, or would he go in and give her a hand, also personally examine sell-by dates, feel plums, etcetera?
                                        Tracy Pakenham, Wimborne

This poser is somewhat trickier than it appears. Normally, Royal Personages try to keep well away from supermarkets because of having to walk round them slowly with their hands behind their backs, manifesting a passionate interest in numbers of chops sold, the technology of coffee granules, the secret of stacking bean tins, the exciting challenge of new bar-codings, and how they manage to find fish with fingers.

Since, however, this is to be a marriage like any other, the radiant couple will naturally be expected to shop for their weekly provisions; certain steps, though, have already been taken to embrace this innovatory move within acceptable protocols.

A State Trolley has been commissioned, narrow enough to pass between supermarket aisles and pulled by four Shetland geldings selected for their continence by the Comptroller of Gastrology to the Royal Mews. Under normal circumstances, this will be driven by the groom while his consort stands on the rear banquette flicking items off the shelves as the Trolley passes with the Shopping Mace of State, a handsome device designed by Asprey's to resemble a gold croupier's rake and incorporating the Chandragore Emerald in its orvidium, now that the curse upon it has been formally removed by the Exorcist General.

Dear Mr Coren:
If he promises to put a shelf up in the kitchen, can she hold him to it if he keeps not getting around to it, also the ball-cock sticking and the overflow going all night?
                                        J. D. Simmons, Hull

Happily, this contingency will never arise. The groom is an avid Do-It-Oneself fanatic, and has personally built an entire maintenance staff, using only a wallet.

Dear Mr Coren:
When they have a right royal row, will they throw things, if so what, and where does she go back to when she walks out? Also, are the neighbours allowed to go round and inform them that some people are trying to sleep?
G. Farris. Cockfosters

Under the 1667 Act of Enragement, originally drawn up to cover the consequences attendant upon any person being discovered bearing oranges in the Royal Apartments, provision is made for the mutual hurling of anything from oaths and accusations to ornaments and dentures.

These are, however, not thrown by the Royal Personages themselves, for obvious reasons. It would not do for a Royal Personage turning up to open a new geriatric wing or launch a frigate to be seen sporting a black eye or swollen hooter.

What happens is that, at the first hint of a raised Royal voice, the Earhole-in-Waiting stationed in the outer office immediately summons the Master of the Queen's Barney, who despatches his two assistants, Hammer Extraordinary and Tongs Puissante, to the Royal quarters, where the Earhole-in-Waiting apprises them of the nature of the row.

It is then fought to a conclusion in front of the Royal couple, each of whom, under the 1667 Act, is bound by the result.

Should the worst come to the worst, it is thus either Tongs who goes home to her mother, or Hammer who goes up the pub.

As to the matter of neighbours, the latest young couple will start their married life in Buckingham Palace, so the question does not arise, unless of course HM the Landlady is herself disturbed, in which case the Keeper of the Privy Shoe may be summoned to bang on the wall.

Softly, a Word or Two Before You Go

AS WE stand trembling, you and I, at the challenging frontier of the New Travel Year, there is but one question to be asked.

Are we going to let Cary Cooper strap a telemeter to our shin?

He is unquestionably qualified to do so, though you could be forgiven for thinking otherwise. From his name, you might not unreasonably induce that he was a blend of two potent cultural icons, and imagine him to be either a sophisticated cowpoke or a mounted gigolo. Indeed, he may well be. What he does on his day off is not our affair.

What he does on his day on, however, is. Cary Cooper's work is to investigate our play. He is, when not roping debutantes or seducing steers, a professor of psychology at the University of Manchester's Institute of Science and Technology, and it was there, as history will record, that he recently sat down and had a bit of a think about things, and came to the conclusion that holidays were bad for you.

Or, more specifically, bad for us. Cary, in common with most shrinks wishing to make an impact on the lay populace, has, according to the scientific journal I have before me, split his research fodder into Two Distinct Types, thus ensuring that every single person lying outside his Manchester moat will instantly hurtle for a pencil stub to measure himself against Cary's arbitrary parameters.

Let me save you the trouble. His two types are A and B. Type A is dynamic, goal-oriented and clever. Type A is ambitious, achieving and highly organized. Type A is a winner.

Type A, in short, is the archetypal *Bin Ends* reader.

Sound good, all those admirable characteristics? Pleased with yourself? Good old Cary Cooper, head screwed on right for a shrink, knows me to a T, or at least an A?

Forget it. Type A is, I have to tell you, the type not to be. Type A is the type who is going to get the telemeter strapped on him.

Because for Type A, holidays are a nightmare.

Let us, before we come to ourselves, read between Professor Cooper's spare lines and examine Type B.

Type B, dim, rut-stuck, motiveless, overdrawn, odd socks, busted fly-zip, rope round suitcase, daft asymmetrical grin girt with shaving-nicks, pimply conk hung with sellotaped sunglasses, Type B ambles cheerfully off to Spain with a plastic bagful of zlotys, an out-of-date passport, an Agatha Christie with the last page missing, and the vague feeling that Gatwick is somewhere near Felixstowe. Behind him, his latchkey remains in his front door, three taps are running, and the fading sound he can't quite put his finger on is his dog barking in the back bedroom.

Despite all this, he nevertheless manages to get himself deposited on roughly the right Costa, where the half of the hotel so far built is subsiding slowly into the car park, and there is no record of his reservation. Mrs Type B, owing to some mix-up over the tickets provided by an agency which has now gone bust, is making her slow and uncomprehending way to Kuala Lumpur by charabanc, and of his three children there is no sign at all, although he has a dim recollection of their having had a cordon sanitaire thrown round them by Spanish immigration officials and a yellow flag going up over the airport.

Type B, however, does not give a monkey's. Type B is on holiday. Type B is going to enjoy himself. Type B is determined to eat, drink and be merry. Pausing only to hand his punctured suitcase to what he assumes, from the mask and striped jersey, to be a porter, he trots to the restaurant, breaks a tooth on a gravelly paella, anaesthetizes it with a jug of rancid sangria at the bottom of which he is much amused to find a drowned cockroach, and goes off, whistling cheerfully through his new cavity, to fry himself blistered on the sewered beach.

Meanwhile, what is happening to Type A, i.e. us? Let me further embellish Professor Cooper's gaunt demographics, just a mite.

Type A, being packed to the gunwales with the intelligence, motivation and organizational capacity that has taken him to the senior board in only five short but goal-oriented years, has driven off for Dover in his just-serviced BMW. He has not only four, but five new tyres, he has not only yellow lenses on his headlamps to placate the Vieux Bill, but also little black stickers gummed to them to comply with Continental dipping variances. His Blaupunkt is pre-programmed to French weather and road information stations, he has a spare windscreen, a red triangle, and a pack of RCMP emergency rations in the boot. His GB plate is luminous.

The spotless Regency house dwindling in the wing-mirrors newly adjusted to conform with EEC Regulation 801/655/b gives no sign either of absentee ownership or the fact that it is a-bristle with the most sophisticated security technology available. Lights wink on and off behind its bazooka-proof windows with cunning irregularity, several tape-recorders are either talking to one another or snoring, and the barking of two Dobermanns is moving electronically from room to room. Needless to say, not only have papers and milk been cancelled, but, because of his farsighted practice of dealing with eight different newsagents and six different dairies on a time-eccentric basis, there is nothing to suggest to anyone that this cancellation betokens absence.

Should any of his four burglar alarm systems trigger during that absence, police from five counties will instantly converge on the house, only to find that the SAS are already abseiling down from the roof.

His real dogs are, of course, kennelled, as is his daughter's hamster and his son's frog. As for his tropical fish, an unimaginably expensive servo-assisted hopper has been installed beside their tank to ensure regular feeding. It is also equipped with a tin arm activated by an electronic eye sensitive to any fish suddenly turning belly-up and becoming a health hazard to its ex-chums. In this event, the arm will whip the little corpse from the water, and bin it.

Needless to say, the entire family has been inoculated against anything that the best hotel on the Riviera can throw at them, and covered by insurance so comprehensive that even a relatively common contingency – such as, say, satellite-fragments falling into their bouillabaisse and staining their bikinis – will immediately produce by return of post an undisputed cashier's cheque equivalent to the GNP of Norway.

Nor has Type A forgotten about his office. Everything that needs to be concealed from prying eyes has been locked in a laser-proof safe, the combination of which he changed ten minutes before leaving. Everything that needs to be revealed to prying eyes has been left lying around with the strategic haphazardness of which he is a past master. His five smartest, most motivated, and most trusted subordinates will have private detectives on them round the clock.

All, in short, has been taken care of, and it will therefore come as no surprise to the *Bin Ends* readership which shares Type A's exemplary meticulousness that by the time he is roughly forty kilometres south of Boulogne, Type A is a nervous wreck. Type A has a lot on what remains of his mind.

Suppose, for example, that the tin arm develops (due, say, to a freak and National-Grid-unsettling thunderstorm) a minor imperfection, so that the dead guppy – a cardiac arrest, perhaps, brought on by its innocence of lightning – misses the waste-bin and strikes instead one of the tape-recorders? Might this produce an effect of barking guests or, worse, snoring guard-dogs?

What if his action in changing the combination of his safe alerts his fellow boardmembers to the possibility of incipient paranoia?

By the time Type A arrives at his hotel (if, indeed, he has not done a handbrake turn at Abbeville and hared shrieking homewards), he is gravely unstitched. His son has a black eye, his daughter has spat out three thousand quids' worth of orthodontic ingenuity, and his wife – following an overnight stop at a pre-booked five-star hostelry where Type A found that the soap-scent was not as specified and fell, weeping hysterically, to the bathroom floor – has put herself in the capable hands of Maître Duclos, the sharpest divorce lawyer in all Bourgogne.

And thereafter, every setback to expectation, however tiny, every pea beneath the mattress, every wasp in the hotel pool, every pre-emptive German towel upon the poolside lounger, every pip in the *tarte aux pommes*, every misunderstood order or misplaced decimal on the barbill will hammer the Type A holidaymaker further up the scale towards the point at which the bell clangs and the Consul has no other option but to arrange for a canvas jacket and a standby flight out.

It is to log all this that Cary Cooper wants to attach a telemeter to Type A's hypertensive person. A telemeter is a little box that measures stress intake. Type A would be telemetrized before he took his 1987 holiday, during it, and, provided he was still around for the telemeter to tell the tale, afterwards. The data would then be codified, pumped into a computer, and, nanoseconds later, provide Professor Cooper with a list of people whom he believes should never go on holiday again.

And how wrong he would be.

For the entire edifice of the research will have been erected upon a false foundation. Which is, quite simply, that stressful and disastrous holidays are bad for the Type A tripper. Nothing could be further from the truth. What are a few days of high blood-pressure, sunstroke, gastritis, peculiar rashes, sleeplessness, insensate rage and expensive disappointment compared with the immeasurable rewards attendant upon finally escaping from them? For us Type A victims, it is absolutely essential that the three weeks snatched as relief be immeasurably more dreadful than the forty-nine we left behind. How on earth could we live with the possibility that what we are not doing might be better than what we do?

Come next summer, I shall gladly bolt on a Manchester telemeter, if Professor Cooper will have me. And I shall pray for my experiences to be such that when he comes to take it off again, it has been fused to clinker.

Someone to Watch Over Me?

'. . . to ring is 01-875 0855. But let's go straight over to Studio 3, where Dennis has now dropped his trousers. Dennis?'

'Thank you, Nick. As you can see, viewers, I am now bending over and looking *through* my legs *into* the mirror. This thing in my left hand is called a haemmorhoscope, and by gently moving aside the things in my right hand, I can use the little torchbulb effort to cast any swollen venous tissue into shadow. You do not *need* a haemmorhoscope, by the way, an ordinary kitchen spatula is just as effective, provided you tie one of those titchy penlights to it of the kind we saw Esther using just a moment ago in the Earwatch studio to look for Eustachian warts. Do, though, remember to sterilize the spatula beforehand, since there is always a risk, however small, of introducing microscopically tiny mouldy food particles into the highly sensitive perineal area, which could possibly give rise to boils that, if unattended, might produce a more generalized septicaemia.'

'Could that make anything fall off, Dennis?'

'Yes, Fiona, it could, and if any viewers have had this experience, or think they may be about to have it, or know of anyone who had it but might for some silly reason not want to phone us themselves, we do urge them to call the Pilewatch number as soon as possible. The number to ring is 01, if you're outside London, 875 0860, and the lines are open now.'

'That's good to know, Dennis. Dennis, this simple little examination, is it safe to do with pets in the room?'

'If the animal is well-behaved, there should be no risk at

all, Fiona. Swollen venous tissue is not contagious, certainly between human beings and domestic animals, but if viewers have any doubts any the excitability of their pet when presented with its owner in an unfamiliar pose, they would be well-advised to ring the Petwatch studio on 01, if they're outside London, 875 0865.'

'Are the lines open now, Dennis?'

'Yes, they are, Fiona. In fact, while I carry on poking about and waiting for calls, why don't we go over to Sue and Roger in the Petwatch studio right now and check that out, Sue?'

'Thank you, Dennis. As a matter of fact, we *have* received a number of calls from pet owners whose animals became disturbed during yesterday's Gutterwatch . . .'

'. . . a loved one falling off the roof will often destabilize an older cat or dog, will it not, Sue?'

'Yes, Roger, and it can't hurt to remind viewers who may think they have a rusty bracket or faulty stepladder, or think they know someone who has something like that, to be sure to lock up any household pet before embarking on their investigation.'

'That would be along with a plentiful supply of food no doubt, Sue?'

'Yes, it would, Roger. Just in case the owner is unfortunate enough to be taken off to the hospital or crematorium.'

'Or perhaps madhouse?'

'Exactly so, Roger. As we saw on Nutwatch last week, many people do not realize they are mentally disturbed until this is triggered off by an unexpected shock, such as falling off a roof. One small but important point – a note left on the door explaining exactly where the pet is locked is a good idea. But, remember, only do it in a code you have agreed upon with your neighbours or the executors of your will, or in a peculiar language you may be lucky enough to have in common, e.g. Samoan, say, or Pawnee, because we do not want to alert burglars to the fact that the householder is in the bin or furnace, do we?'

'No, Sue, I think that was made very clear on a recent Crimewatch, as a quick call to 01, if you're outside London, 875 0875 will verify. The lines are open now. Sue, about this enquiry of Dennis's concerning pets being disturbed by Pilewatch examinations – I've just been passed this note by one of our lovely telephone ladies saying they've had a call from a gentleman in Runcorn wishing to know if a bite from his upset pussy could give him herpes. Any views?'

'Not my field, I'm afraid, Roger, I think I'd like to go straight across to the Rashwatch studio for Jonathan's expert comments on this one. Jonathan?'

'Thank you Sue, hallo viewers, and, by the way, I see from my monitor that Dennis seems to have found something, but more of that anon. The short answer to the gentleman from Runcorn, Sue, is that neither herpes nor, come to that, AIDS, can be caught from a cat's bite, unless you're very, very unlucky indeed and the cat has bitten a carrier less than five minutes earlier. What our Runcorn viewer ought to worry about, perhaps, as should many of us, is rabies, which, of course, is untreatable and means you die in excruciating agony screaming out for water. But that's an amateur view, Sue – I'd be much happier transferring you to Sally and Geoff in the Chunnelwatch studio. Sally?'

'Hallo, Jonathan.'

'Hallo, Jonathan.'

'Hallo, Geoff. I assume your lines are open?'

'Yes, Jonathan, on 01, if you're outside London, 875, 0880. And even as we speak, those lines, I hear from the producer, are jammed with calls from viewers in Kent worried about dying in excruciating agony and screaming for water when the Channel Tunnel opens.'

'Are they right to worry, Geoff?'

'Put it this way, Sally, if I lived within a hundred miles of the Channel Tunnel entrance, I would be off out of there like a rat up a drain!'

'Because of the rats up the drain, Geoff?'

'Exactly so, Sally, har-har-har! The first train coming over from France will make Hamelin look like a vicarage tea-party. The little buggers will be hanging out of the windows and waving, if I'm any judge.'

'Especially, I assume, if they have gnawed their way into sacks of certain substances being smuggled in from the Middle East lashed to the bogies, as we were recently warned on Drugwatch, Railwatch and Wogwatch was bound to happen?'

'Spot on, Sally!'

'And could there really be a risk to a cat in Runcorn?'

'No question. Rabies, once endemic, spreads faster than you can blink. As a matter of fact, I was discussing this with Olive in the Plaguewatch studios, and it is her professional opinion, after more than three full weeks as a presenter, that it is even money whether HTLV3 or rabies wipes out the country first.'

'Good heavens! Even money?'

'So she claims, Jonathan, although I gather that Ladbroke's are still offering 7-4 against rabies, but you'll have to be quick. The number to ring is 01, if you're outside London, 459 8031. The lines are open now, and if you feel like a flutter on an outsider, you might try a bob or two on the Hong Kong Gamma-16 virus! I was watching it work out this morning under the Fluwatch microscope, and it could surprise everybody.'

'Thanks for the tip, Geoff. As a matter of fact, I've just had a flash from the Plaguewatch studio myself, Olive would like any viewer who thinks he or she has, or knows anyone who thinks he or she has, a bubo, to have a good feel under their arms and ring her on 01, if they're outside London, 875 0885.'

'Hang about, Jonathan, surely that falls within the purview of Lumpwatch? What do you think, Geoff?'

'Yes, I'm afraid I should have to back Sally there, Jonathan. There is a great risk here, surely, of viewers suddenly ringing up Plaguewatch with any old lump. The proper course is to phone Lumpwatch first on 01, if they're outside London, 875 0890, and get expert advice from Desmond or Noel, who, if it is a bubo, will then be able to refer them to Olive for specialist opinion. Can you confirm that, Desmond or Noel?'

'Hallo, Geoff, sorry, we are up to here on Lumpwatch, that is the problem with general practice, we have got crackpots jamming the switchboard with everything from warts to molehills, never mind illiterates trying to get through to Limpwatch, you would not believe the backlog, we could not touch anything new for three months. I have it on good authority, mind, that things are a bit slow over in the Bumpwatch studio, now that cranial swellings and other contusions are being dealt with by Spousebatterwatch, and our colleagues Nat and Hazel are therefore generously prepared to take viewers' calls on underarm excrescences – though they stress that they are acting solely as a temporary clearing-house – on 01, if you're outside London, 875 0895. Okay, Nat?'

'Spot on, Desmond, but can I just remind viewers that

Hazel and I will continue to take car-damage calls, provided they are genuine coachwork queries and not of an engineering nature, which should be addressed, as always, to Funnyknockingwatch, where the lines are open on 01, if you're outside London, 875 0900.'

'Thanks for the reminder, Nat, many viewers, I know, have been ringing Funnyknockingwatch with enquiries regarding double-glazing, Jehovah's Witnesses, the *Encyclopaedia Britannica*, and so forth, and I would ask these viewers to please, *please*, consult the correct numbers on Ceefax before placing an unnecessary burden on our overworked operators. Thinking of which, I'm getting an urgent signal from Norman in the Watchwatch studio. Norman?'

'Hallo, Desmond, sorry to cut in, but an unprecedented number of disease-ridden viewers have been ringing Watchwatch to say that they have become convinced that many of their neighbours may be homicidal maniacs with contagious lumps, bumps, or limps, and that any minute now they and their rabid cats will begin breaking in and battering their drug-crazed children, and who can they turn to for help before it's too late? Well, since we seem to be getting more and more of these sorts of call from frantic viewers, you'll be relieved to know we've set up a special hot line to deal with them! The number to ring is 01, if you're . . .

Mine Eyes Have Seen the Glory

YOU WILL, I feel certain, forgive the blanking out of my address. You may be only a commoner, but it does not necessarily follow that you are a numskull. Some of my best friends were commoners, in the past, and I know whereof I speak.

We lords cannot be too careful about our addresses. Put

one's address about uncircumspectly, and one would not believe the Toms, Dicks and Harries coming round on the earhole, one would be handing out florins all day. Nor does it behove us lords to tell Jehovah's double-glazers etcetera to urinate off, one has to stand there and beam at the buggers, it is called *noblesse oblige*, as I understand.

Anyway, I shall not have the address for much longer. You cannot live at 26 anything, as a lord: you have to live at places called Jobsworth or Knackers or Saucepans. You cannot have a postcode, either; it is common as muck, having EC4 2FH after your name, you have to have *of* something, e.g. Rievaulx, or The Hirsel, or That Ilk. They have not told me what mine is yet, it has not been graciously vouchsafed to me where I am Lord Coren of, could be Cricklewood, could be 23-27 Tudor Street, it'll probably come with the second post, I shall keep an eye on the mat.

I shall almost certainly call the house Oddbins, mind. I am given to understand that that is the way it goes in the honours business. They are all men of the world. There would not be all this current unsavoury argy-bargy up the High Court if Robert Maxwell had, let us say, done all his shopping at the right place, he would have his feet under the table at Tesco Manor by now, Viscount Maxwell of Bingo, for example.

I do not know exactly how Oddbins swung it, of course. I may be a member of the Establishment, but that does not mean I am privy, yet, to everything that goes on in the corridors of power. It was probably a question of the manager of the Belsize Park branch having friends at the Palace, or being Supplier of Pork Scratchings to the Prime Minister, or some such; that is the way these things work, every year he looks down the list of favoured customers and anyone who has clocked up more than, say, forty cases of brown ale is in for an MBE, and on up to Earldoms.

I got through a lot of Glenfiddich in 1985, which probably explains it. Just shows you it is always worth forking out a bit extra for single malts, if I'd stuck to Johnny Walker Red Label I'd probably be nothing more than a knight, today.

They are extremely influential, vintners. It is a well-known fact. If you are a Queen or Prime Minister, you have to keep on the right side of your supplier; there is nothing worse than getting, for example, a state visit from the Akond of Swat and watching his first swig of the '61 pucker his face like a prune. Vintners have had their foot in the best doors for centuries. John Chaucer, you will recall, was a top wine merchant, which explains how Geoffrey wangled his way to Court, also got a good seat on the coach, if I'm any judge.

I was, despite all this, a bit surprised at the manner of what I took to be the official announcement. I had rather expected a big bit of ochre vellum with 𝔅𝔢 𝔍𝔱 𝔎𝔫𝔬𝔴𝔫 𝔅𝔶 𝔗𝔥𝔢𝔰𝔢 𝔓𝔞𝔱𝔢𝔫𝔱 𝔗𝔥𝔞𝔱 𝔚𝔢 𝔄𝔯𝔢 𝔊𝔯𝔞𝔠𝔦𝔬𝔲𝔰𝔩𝔶 𝔓𝔩𝔢𝔞𝔰𝔢𝔡 𝔗𝔬 . . . and so forth, preferably horse-drawn to the house by a couple of periwigged buglers in cloth-of-gold pinnies, if only to give the window-cleaner something to put in his memoirs; but in the event the intelligence was merely fisted through the letter-box in the normal way, an hour ago. You would have thought, at least, that the postman would have rung the bell and handed the thing over on his knees.

I stared at the envelope for some time. I may have rolled the inscription around on my tongue for a bit. *Lord Coren* has a not unengaging ring. Very good for getting a table near the band or being caught doing ninety on Hendon Way. When I picked it up, however, the envelope, though encouragingly 10 by 8 and buff, seemed to me a little light for an Official Announcement – they had clearly not enclosed the blazer-badge, tie, or ferret-samples for the collar. I had a bit of a feel round between thumb and forefinger to see if there was a peer's tie-pin or crested ball-point or anything, but no joy.

So I opened it.

And, as you can see, it was not an announcement at all. Simply a matter of Oddbins jumping the gun. I should have twigged that there's a good two months to go yet before the New Year's Honours List, it's clear what's happened, Oddbins has put my name forward, got the nod from the Honours Office, taken it as read, put me on the Favoured Customer list, and forgotten that I have not yet been Officially Approached.

Not that I mind. I should not wish Oddbins to go about biting their knuckles at the thought that they have incurred my gracious displeasure. I shall not be slapping any 1346 statutes on them for malfeasance or scrimshaw or turvery or anything of that order, which I shall doubtless be empowered to do upon delivery of coronet and bumper-sticker. Quite the contrary, given that they are so generously prepared to bung me on their Favoured Customer list and enclose my Privilege Card several weeks before Her Majesty has even got her rubber stamp out.

It is quite amazing what you come in for as a peer of the realm. According to their letter, production of the Privilege Card gets you 14p off White Satin Gin, 26p off Baileys Irish Cream, and a full quid off a bottle of Remy Martin! And how about this:

> Each time you visit an Oddbins store between 3rd November and 28th November 1986 you will receive a ticket on which should be written your name, address and telephone number. The ticket should be placed in the box provided and if your name is drawn on Saturday 29th November you win the chance to have a 30-second dash around the store. Everything you can grab during that time, subject to the competition rules, is yours!

What an astonishing glimpse behind the aristocratic arras is afforded by this gobbet! It is like looking through a masonic keyhole, the mystic veil is lifted, scales fall from the eyes – who could have guessed that such arcane rights went with ennoblement? When I was a commoner, all I thought they got was £54 attendance allowance, Black Rod to open the back door, and, in the unlikely event these days of their patch still having a virgin on it, the spasmodic option of seigneurial leg-over. I never realized they could be graciously vouchsafed a thirty-second free go in the Oddbins November Handicap – what visions are conjured up of Willie Whitelaw, laden with crates of Cockburns Special Reserve yet still managing to take Douglas-Home on the final turn, due to the latter's having failed to vault a prone Forte brought down by rolling magnums of Soave left in the wake of the fast-hobbling Runcie, but finally thwarted at the till by Hailsham's malacca cane thrust deftly between his twinkling calves!

And it is, as I say, only a glimpse. Who can guess what other privileged goodies will be tumbling through the flap from now on? What free aristocratic leg-waxings, nobs-only crystal goblet offers, belted Black Sea weekends, what patrician carwash tokens, noble loft-conversion deals, exclusive opportunities to examine Melvyn's new novel in the privacy of my own seat, without obligation?

One conundrum remains. I do not know what political colour I am supposed to be. According to *The Times* which lies beside my Oddbins letter as I type, 'with the opening of the new parliamentary session, Neil Kinnock is expected to make his formal approach to Margaret Thatcher for up to six appointments to increase the Labour Party's strength in the House of Lords. Mrs Thatcher, however, will insist on matching the new Labour peers with about six Tory life peers.'

Clearly, I am one of these, submitted by Oddbins, nodded through by the Palace, and awaiting only my gazetting. But to whom did Oddbins submit me, Kinnock or Thatcher?

Not, I suppose, that it matters much. I am, after all, an English nobleman, and above such things. Give me five bob off a bottle of Tio Pepe and a couple of decent stalls for *Cats*, and Her Majesty may do with me what she will.

Smiling Through

Computer scientists in California believe they have evidence that the Mona Lisa was originally wearing a necklace.

Dr John Asmus, who headed a team which investigated the picture using computer image analysis techniques, told yesterday's annual meeting of the American Association for the Advancement of Science that Leonardo da Vinci probably changed his mind about the portrait and painted over the necklace.

the Independent

'HALLO!' SHOUTED Leonardo da Vinci, into the cocoa tin. 'Is that Florence 2?'

He put the tin to his ear.

From somewhere deep inside came a sound not unlike a cockroach running through iron filings. He took his ear out of the tin again.

'Speak up!' he shouted.

The tin squawked, unintelligibly.

He pulled on the string. Beyond his attic dormer, it tautened above the umber roofscape, scattering sparrows. He was about to put the tin to his ear again, when the string went suddenly slack.

'Sod it,' said Leonardo.

He put the cocoa tin back on his desk, and ran out of his studio, slamming the door. Caught in the slipstream of his flying cloak, a preliminary cartoon for *The Battle of Anghiari* trembled on his easel, floated to the floor, and came to rest face up. The moted sunlight fell across two battered Medici grenadiers crouching in a muddy crater. *'If you knows of a better 'ole . . .'* the caption began; but, like so much else these days, it was unfinished, and would in all likelihood remain so.

On the landing, Leonardo sprang into the lift, plummeted, screamed, and was hurled off his feet as it stopped without warning between floors. He rang the emergency handbell, and was winched slowly down by a bloomered pupil.

'Up the spout,' muttered Leonardo.

'*Up the spout*, Master?' murmured the pupil.

'It is a technical phrase I have invented,' replied Leonardo da Vinci, straightening his plume, 'to describe lifts.'

'Is it like *on the blink*, Master?' enquired the pupil.

'No,' said Leonardo. '*On the blink* describes telephones.'

'Is Florence 1 on the blink again, then?'

'Yes. There is a fault on the line. It is my opinion the knot has come out of Florence 2.'

'It is nevertheless,' said the pupil, simpering warmly, 'a wonderful invention, and a boon to man!'

'Inventing the cocoa tin was the hard part,' said Leonardo. He sniffed, bitterly. 'You would think that once you'd come up with the cocoa tin, it would all be downhill after that. You would think the string would be a doddle. It's a bugger, science. Half the time, it makes no bloody sense at all.' He pushed into the new revolving door which led to his workshop, and the pupil pushed in behind him. After about ten minutes of banging and shrieking, the pupil came out in front.

'Up the blink, Master?' murmured the pupil, gloomily watching Leonardo's shredded cloak smouldering in the door's boiler. 'On the spout?'

'Down the tubes,' muttered Leonardo. He dusted himself off, and peered into the bustling workshop, on the far side of which a tiny buskinned man was throwing vegetables into a large glass cylinder. 'Hallo, what's that little twerp Giovanni up to now?'

The pupil examined his clipboard.

'Where are we?' he said. 'Tuesday, Tuesday, yes, Tuesday he is supposed to be on rotary-wing research. He is down here as developing the Leonardo Gnat.'

Cursing, Leonardo ran across and snatched an imminent

cucumber from Giovanni's little hands; in the confusion, a chicken scrambled out of the glass cylinder and fled, clucking.

'That's never a helicopter!' cried Leonardo.

'Insofar as you would have a job getting to Pisa in it,' replied the pupil, 'that is true. However, Master, it works on the same principle. It is what we call a spin-off. If I may be permitted?'

Leonardo prodded the cylinder with his patent umbrella. The ferrule droped off.

'Two minutes,' he said. 'But God help you if it turns out to be another bloody toaster. They'll never send the fire brigade out four days in a row.'

Giovanni, who had meanwhile been turning a large key protruding from the base of the cylinder, now took a deep breath, and flicked a switch. Inside the cylinder, blades whirled, howling; a white lumpy mass spread across the ceiling. Leonardo looked slowly up, as the substance coalesced into soft stalactites; a blob fell into his beard, and he licked it off.

'Vichyssoise, is it?' he enquired, levelly.

'Leek and turnip, actually,' said Giovanni. He spooned a quantity from Leonardo's hat, and tasted it. 'Could do with a bit more garlic?'

Leonardo swung his umbrella. It turned, naturally enough, inside out, but the residual sturdiness was still enough to fell Giovanni where he stood. Slowly, his ear swelled, glowing.

'I want this one,' said Leonardo to the pupil-foreman, 'on the next train to Santa Maria della Grazie.'

'*The Last Supper*, Master?' cried the pupil-foreman, aghast. 'Are you sure he's up to it?'

'I'm a dab hand with apostles,' retorted Giovanni, struggling to his feet, 'also glassware. You could drink out of my goblets.'

'He will not be painting the wall,' said Leonardo, 'he will be plastering it prior to undercoat, as per ours of the 14th ultimo, plus removing all rubbish from site and making good.'

'Bloody hell!' cried Giovanni. 'All I forgot was the lid! I have not even mentioned the fact that the amazing new Vincimix comes with a range of attachments which chop, shred, slice, and whip the pips out of a quince before you can

100

say Jack Robinson.'

At which point, all the windows blew in.

Slowly, Leonardo da Vinci walked through the settling dust, and looked out. A blackened face looked back at him. Neither spoke. Leonardo turned and walked back through the room.

'You'll have to go by horse,' he said to Giovanni.

'Do not be downcast, Master,' said the pupil-foreman. 'Nobody said trains were easy.'

Leonardo stared at the floor.

'Funny,' he said, 'the lid hops up and down all right on the kettle.'

The clock struck ten. Absently, Leonardo picked up the fallen cuckoo, walked out of the workshop, into the sunlit street, climbed on his bicycle, and began pedalling slowly towards Fiesole, scattering nuts and spokes. By the time he reached the house of Zanoki del Giocondo, he was carrying a wheel and a saddlebag, and sweating.

He tugged the bell-rope.

'I phoned,' he gasped, when she answered the door.

'The knot came out,' she replied.

'I thought so,' he said. He cleared his throat. 'Is he in?'

'He's out in his tank.'

'I thought he'd like that,' said Leonardo. 'I thought it might get him out of the house.' He walked into the hall. 'I hope he doesn't suspect anything, mind.'

'No. He thinks you're a faggot. Nobody else gives him presents.' A neighbour passed, and peered, and smiled. La Gioconda nodded, and closed the front door. 'How long is he likely to stay out?' she said. 'I don't know anything about tanks.'

'Days, possibly,' said Leonardo. 'We haven't cracked this business of the tracks. It tends to go round in circles until the engine seizes up. Even if he manages to get the lid open again, he won't have the faintest idea where he is.'

'But we ought to do a bit more of the painting, first?'

'You can't be too careful,' said Leonardo da Vinci. He propped his wheel against the dado, and opened his saddlebag, and took out his palette and his easel; but as he was following her through the house and out into the garden – not simply for the light but for the assuaging of neighbourly curiosity – he could not help noticing the way a sunbeam fell across her plump shoulder, and the way her hips rolled.

So they decided to do a bit more of the painting afterwards, instead.

And when they were in the garden, finally, he put the necklace around her neck, and fastened the clasp, and she cried aloud:

'Diamonds!'

'What else?' he said.

So she sat in her chair, with her hands folded and a broad smile on her tawny face, and Leonardo da Vinci's brushes flicked back and forth, and the neighbours peered from between the mullions, and were satisfied.

And then it began to rain.

Not seriously enough to drive them in; just a warm summer blob or two. But one such, unfortunately, fell on her necklace, and, after a few moments, she looked down, and stared; and then she said, carefully:

'The diamonds appear to be going grey.'

'Ah,' said Leonardo.

'Is that usual?'

Leonardo came out from behind his easel, and looked at them.

'It could be,' he said, 'With this new process.'

'I'm sorry?'

'It's a bit technical,' said Leonardo.

'Try me.'

'You start off with coal,' said Leonardo.

'I see.'

She stared at him for a long while after that, until Leonardo went back behind his easel. He picked up his brush.

He looked at her.

Her lip curled.

He put the brush down again.

'It isn't much of a smile,' said Leonardo da Vinci.

'It isn't much of a necklace,' said Mona Lisa.

Diabolical Liberties

*Halloween has traditionally been believed to be the most
favourable opportunity for divinations concerning marriage,
luck, health, prosperity, and so on. It is the only day on which the
help of the devil may be invoked for such purposes.*

Encyclopaedia Britannica

Dear Prince of Darkness,
I am 42 years old and have been married for 19 years to my
husband Monty, now a Senior Sales Manager with responsibility for a wide range of executive patio novelties. Having
two bathrooms, one ensuite, and my own Datsun Loganberry GL as well as three children, I think it is, I have always
counted myself very fortunate, but of late my marriage
seems to have been going through a rough patch. My
husband's duties frequently mean he is not home until
nearly *Dallas*, he often eats his dinner without even looking
at it, and for our last anniversary he gave me an all-weather
draining-board, which I know for a fact is one of the lines he
is having trouble shifting.
  Have you any suggestions?

Cheryl, Woking

Dear Cheryl,

Marriage is a contract between two people for better or worse, requiring give and take, sharing and caring, and the need to face life's myriad problems together. Those entering into it should therefore accept that their heads need examining.

My expert opinion is that Monty has twigged that you are over the hill, and is having it away with some big leggy blonde half your age. My professional advice, since he does not look at his dinner, is to lace it with rat poison for a few days, stick him in the back of the Datsun before he stiffens up, and dump him in some handy spot, e.g. nearby reservoir, pot-hole, or similar, and get on to his insurance company. That done, your wisest course would be to smother yourself in cheap scent and start hanging around rugby clubs while you still have a bit of tread on you.

Dear Prince of Darkness,
I am at my wit's end. I am 53 years old and have worked as a counter clerk for the Abbey National Building Society for 30 years without a single day off, including my dear mother's funeral where we kept her hanging about until August Bank Holiday so as not to inconvenience, and Marmite sandwiches on premises every lunchtime to avoid risk of being late back due to new batch of Big Macs not up yet etcetera, and what with this impeccable record and everything, I was fully expecting to step into Mr Foskett's shoes upon his retirement as Branch Manager, another £28.34 per week, plus own frosted-glass cubicle.

But they have only gone and given it to Winston Wellington, haven't they, due to misguided equal opportunities codswallop, hardly been with us three years, Head Office say he has a warm and welcoming smile, but that is only because their teeth show up better. I took my letter to the pub next door after locking the safe last night in order to celebrate with a cider, only when I opened it there was sod all except a round robin trusting I would continue to give sterling service under the new manager.

I have put a down-payment on a night-storage heater in expectation of a rise, and I do not know where to turn. Can you suggest a part-time job or anything?

Harold, Tufnell Park

Dear Harold,
Yes. The best part-time job would be to tunnel in from the cellar of the pub next door. Being granted custody of the keys puts you in a position of great trust and means you could go through that safe like a pint of Eno's. They would never suspect you, especially as you could put the finger on Winston by leaving a water melon or ghetto-blaster lying about, thereby killing two birds with one stone!

If, however, you do not feel up to swinging a pick all night, I could put you in touch with Cheryl of Woking, who is a hardened criminal and would almost certainly be prepared to come in with a stocking over her head and a shotgun, take the keys off you, turn the safe over, and split the difference, due to where she will find herself a bit short any day now upon discovery that her husband's insurance company is unlikely to cough up in suspicious circumstances.

An added bonus is that you could well be in for a bit of legover there, if I know Cheryl. I'd keep the stocking over her head, mind, if I were you.

Dear Prince of Darkness,
Wouldn't you know it? The steering on my pacy two-tone Lada Truckette GT has just gone wonky *two weeks after the guarantee ran out*! Is there any way of approaching my local dealer in order to ensure satisfaction?

Kevin, Tottenham

Dear Kevin,
I have looked into this closely, and the most direct way of approaching your local dealer is straight up Osbaldeston Road to the T junction, across the pavement, and through his plate-glass window. If you give it plenty of boot and the steering holds up, you could well wipe out four or five new models, thus ensuring considerable satisfaction.

However, a more profitable option would be to park it

105

outside the Abbey National office in Tufnell Park and wait for a woman in a stocking mask who will probably be very keen to do a straight swop for a very nice low-mileage Datsun Loganberry GL, the only minor shortcoming of which is a strange smell issuing from the boot which she would probably prefer not to have to account for in the event of the Old Bill stopping her to enquire about the Abbey National sacks on her back seat.

Furthermore, she will very likely throw in a quick one for good measure, if there's time. She is known to be a bit of a goer.

Dear Prince of Darkness,
I am 17 years old, and I have fallen for this really triff-looking girl in Tesco's, long copper barnet, ace legs, but the great thing is she blushes and has this crucifix round her neck, it is my belief she has not yet been mucked about with to speak of. Anyway, I have took the plunge and asked her out tomorrow, and my question is, would she still respect me if I kissed her on our first date?

Jason, Edgware

Dear Jason,
Yes, there is a danger she would. If you want to be on a winner, your best bet is to spend next week hanging around Tufnell Park with a spanner in your hand and keeping your eye open for a two-tone Lada Truckette GT which will be wobbling from side to side, and not difficult to run after on foot.

When it pulls up at the Gospel Oak traffic lights, bang the spanner on the driver's window and inform her that you are a trained Lada mechanic who just happened to be passing and would be delighted to effect repairs to same by driving it into a quiet side street and getting on the job right away.

Since the truckette has no windows in the back, and will be equipped with a couple of comfy seats, I trust I do not have to draw pictures.

Dear Prince of Darkness,

I do not know whether your advice extends to medical matters, but I have been feeling a bit icky this morning, it started soon after last night's *Dallas*. At first I put it down to the shock of Bobby Ewing coming back from the dead – no disrespect intended – but I now think it could be due to wrong eating habits and rushing about all the time, this being our busy period in the executive patio novelty profession. Should I go on to a high-fibre diet, lay off alcohol, and so forth, or what?

Monty, Woking

Dear Monty,

I shouldn't bother, old cock. We only, all right, you only, pass this way but once, and my advice is to have a good time while you can.

It so happens there's a nice fresh long-legged red-head just come on the market, works at the Edgware Tesco's, has recently been stood up by a young toerag, and is very likely in a major rebound situation. An experienced man of the world could be on to a real winner there!

I wouldn't hang about too long, though, if I were you.

True Snails Read (anag., 8,6)

SQUIRE **Walt Reeny**, Dr **Yesvile**, and the rest of these gentlemen having asked me to write down the whole particulars about **True Snails Read?** from the beginning to the end, keeping nothing back but the answers to 14 across and 23 down, and that only because there is treasure still to be lifted, I take up my pen in the year of grace 17--, and go back to the time when my father kept the Admiral Benbow inn, and the brown old seaman with the terrible nib-scar first took up his lodging under our roof.

I remember him as if it were yesterday, as he came plodding to the inn door, his twenty-four salt-caked volumes of the *Oxford English Dictionary* following behind him in a hand-barrow, his high reedy voice breaking out in that old sea-song that was to haunt my dreams:

'Corpse at bottom of scrum! We hear
He's worth more than one small bier!'

I opened the door to him, and he threw himself into a chair, crying:

'A palindrome? Yes, but this one's not for kids, me hearties! It's peculiar.'

I stared at him.

'I beg your pardon, sir?' I said.

'I think,' said my father, from the dark recess of the bar, 'he wants a tot. Of, if I am not mistaken, rum.'

The stranger smote the table.

'Be 'ee a crosswordin' man?' he cried joyously.

My father smiled.

'**4, 4, 1, 4,**' he replied, '**according to the best fairy stories. Not these days, though.**'

The old sailor nodded, and, when my father went out for the bottle, drew me to him with an inky claw, so close that I could see the flecks of chewed quill stuck upon his lip, and smell the indiarubber on his nails.

'Yonder,' he whispered excitedly, nodding towards the bar-window and the broad bay beyond, 'lies the S.S. *Canberra*. I ships aboard 'er on the morrow tide.'

'You are bound for the Crossword Cruise, sir?' I exclaimed. 'You go in search of the Grand Prize? May I wish you the very best of luck?'

'Luck?' cried the old man in a terrible voice. '**Luck's a chance, but ‑‑‑‑‑‑‑'s sure (*Housman*) (7).** I makes my own luck, lad! See this 'ere diddy-box 'o mine?'

I nodded. It was a battered, brassbound thing, with **FLAT CAP, INNIT?** engraved upon the lid.

'Yes,' I said, proud of myself, 'I noticed it immediately. It seemed such a queer shape for a hatbox.'

The old blood-threaded eyes gazed at me as if I were deranged.

'Hatbox?' he muttered. 'That be no hatbox, lad. That be the personal property o' the late –' and here his voice dropped to a cracked whisper '– *Captain Flint!*'

Letters swam in my head. Truth dawned.

'It be why I doan need luck, see?' said the old sailor. His eyes grew moist with more than rheum. 'Flint were the smartest puzzle dog I ever shipped with, lad. Flint knew the Latin handle of every plant that ever were, 'e 'ad the entire *Oxford Dictionary o' Quotes* to heart, 'e could spell backwards in fourteen lingos, 'e knew eight 'undred words wi' two letters in 'em! He dreamed in anagrams, did Flint, he saw acrostics in the stars. I remember one time we was becalmed off the Dry Tortegas, half-mad from heat and thirst and not a man among us capable o' getting 1 across in the *Sun* – **It sat on the mat (3)** – and there were Flint on the after-deck doing the *Telegraph* with 'is left hand and *The Times* with 'is right, while 'is parrot read him the *Guardian* so's he could do it in 'is head simultaneous!'

'Remarkable!' I cried.

'**This rare genus had one eye (6),**' murmured the old man, blowing his nose fiercely on a red bandanna, 'but has now **gone up to meet his dog (3)**.'

'What, then, is in his box?' I enquired.

A dry hand closed over my own, so firmly that I could feel the sharp callus on a forefinger flattened by a million clues.

'Ye seems a lad who would **look after his short mother (4,3)**,' murmured the ancient. 'A year or two back, just after Flint 'ung up 'is sextant, the P&O come to 'im wi' a proposition. Not a sea-dog from Maracaibo to the Cape as 'adn't 'eard tell o' Flint's magic powers, see, an' it were only a matter o' course afore –'

'No need to go on, sir!' I cried. 'I may be a stranger to the cryptic force, but I can divine a drift as well as any! You are telling me that Flint became the brains behind the Crossword Cruise! You are intimating that the incalculable treasure which awaits one brilliant, albeit peculiar, passenger comes with the solution to a Grand Prize Jumbo Puzzle set by –'

My companion spread his hands, nodding.

'**Did the good doctor fail to diagnose his digestive problem? Sounds as though his friend Sherlock has! (10),**' he said.

I pointed excitedly at the diddy-box.

'And this can only mean,' I exclaimed, 'that you have Captain Flint's papers, and therefore the answer to the Canberra's Prize Jum –'

The finger was across my lips. Its tremble was so stricken that my ear-ring shook.

'*What is that strange tapping?*' he croaked.

I searched for the true meaning hidden in this cryptogram, knowing by now that *strange*, like *disturbed, confused, upset,* and so forth, betokened some anagrammatic interference. But what could I make from **tapping**? Was *gnippat* some rare Sumatran weevil, *pantpig* a Jacobean pervert, *Ignappt* the early working-title of something by that drunk Robert Louis Stevenson who lived in our small back room? It was while I was pondering this that I became aware of a noise beyond the window, as of a stick banging rhythmically against the wall.

I glanced at my companion, who had begun to gasp horribly.

'**We see nothing on this church bench! (5,3),**' he managed, finally, to sob.

I swivelled as the inn door burst open; and caught my breath. At first, I saw naught but the white stick that had thrust it wide: but soon thereafter, a squat, malign figure entered the room, a dreadful leer playing beneath the sightless eyes. He tapped his way to our table, and, reaching out a clammy hand, touched my face.

'Pew,' he said. 'I am confused.'

Wep? I thought, *ewp?*

'I had been expecting an old friend but – ah!' he cried, as his hand groped on and suddenly found my companion, cringing in his chair, 'I was not wrong.'

Whereupon he removed a folded scrap of paper from his smock, placed it carefully on the table between us, turned, and made his echoing way out again.

Since my companion seemed too stricken to move, I took the liberty of picking up the scrap and unfolding it. The eyes in the rigid face opposite now flickered in resigned enquiry.

'**Negro Topsy upside down? Don't say why! (5,4),**' I read.

He groaned horribly. A further, deeper shudder racked his ancient frame. His eyes rolled to white. As a drowning man throws up one sinking hand, he beckoned me close.

'**Skin –**' he wheezed, but the rest of the sentence ebbed.

'Go on!' I urged. 'I could not hear!'

He made a supreme and dreadful effort.

'**Skin game – for Cricket Cup?**' he gasped, finally. '**(4,3).**'

I racked such brain as I could muster. The ruin opposite, tongue lolling noiselessly behind cracked lips, could be no help.

And then, clouds parted, light burst through.

'Hide box!' I shouted.

He nodded, just perceptibly.

I snatched up Flint's precious bequest, wrapped it quickly in a tablecloth, rose, and would have left forthwith to seek a spot of suitable impenetrability, had not the dying unfortunate clutched at my urgent sleeve in one last desperate bid.

He pulled, with terminal strength, my ear towards his lip.

'Beware!'

His voice was like an on-shore breeze against the dry grass of the dunes.

'Beware of what?' I said.

The tongue laid a last bead of moisture on the lip.

'Of a seafaring man with one backward gel!' he gasped.
And died.

Next Week's Episode. **Hallmarked underwear? (4,4,6) Why not, if the parrot's good as gold! (6,2,5)**

Fiddler on the Roof

A handy spring guide for those wishing to make good the ravages of the worst winter in roofing memory

Poking Something Dead out of a 4" Soil Elbow Using the Half-hoe and dangling Paperclip Techniques

During the winter, our feathered friends often stand on chimneys, probably to see if there are crumbs in neighbouring gardens. Sometimes, for reasons not always clear to ornithologists, they drop dead, roll down the roof, get lodged in the gutter, and, with the spring thaw, wash into the downpipe and become stuck in the junction with the external soil-pipe, causing unsavoury backwash to sanitary ware and people indoors going around saying 'What's that niff?'

Before, therefore, levering up external drain man-holes with an old hub-cap and poking tied-together golfclubs along the conduits, it is sensible to determine that the fault does not lie with a rotted starling or similar. Go up to the roof-guttering, using an extending ladder and a 137/4b/26 BUPA claim form, and, with a four-foot length of sharpened hoe-handle, poke down hard towards the elbow. With luck, you will impale the corpse and, withdrawing the hoe hand-over-hand, remove it altogether. If you poke too hard, and the downpipe is either plastic or old cast-iron, you may find that the starling comes out through a hole in the elbow, but do not worry, the gap may be quite easily repaired with Harbutt's Plasticine, or, more professionally, with instant glue and a hole-shaped piece of waterproof thingy cut from an old anorak.

If, however, as can happen with any advanced technology, the hoe-handle falls into the downpipe, it may be possible to retrieve the corpse using a piece of ordinary kitchen string with a paperclip affixed to one end and twisted to form a

114

hook. With a fully deteriorated bird, you should be able to lower the hook inside the rib cage and locate it under the sternum; if the feathers and flesh have not yet rotted off, though, try to get the hook around a foot (or 'claw'). It should then draw up easily.

The fallen hoe-handle, in most cases, is best left where it is. The attendant reduction of volume of the downpipe should not cause problems, except in rain, but if water does flood up and over the guttering, it is a simple matter to bang a hole in the guttering and stand an oil drum under it. When emptying the oil drum, do NOT attempt to tip it over (it will weigh half a ton!), simply siphon the water by sucking through a tube cut from garden hose into some other convenient smaller receptacle, such as a tin bath, from which the water may then easily be emptied with a saucepan.

Replacing Blown-off Roof Tiles without Dangerous Hammering

Tiles are attached to roofs by a complicated system of battens, lugs and titchy little tacks that cannot be held by normal human beings without getting a thumb flattened, often the cause of the hammer sliding down the roof and into a downpipe whence, due to its consistency, it cannot of course be removed with a half-hoe or paperclip. You have to prise the entire length of pipe from the brickwork using a garden spade, which may sometimes break in two. If this happens, do not throw the pieces away: the shovel bit can come in useful for lifting a man-hole cover if your hub-cap is not up to it, and the handle bit can be used for breaking up larger birds, e.g. pigeons, storks, etc. that have got into other downpipes and can be removed only after dismembering.

There is, however, an alternative to all this heavy labour on tiles. That is to use common or garden adhesive tape! Simply tape one end to a new tile with a generous length left hanging and – having climbed up your ladder to the lower end of the pitched roof – push the tile up the roof using a long mop (or, if the missing tile is high up, a long mop tied to a broom) until it is over the hole. Then, very carefully, flip up the length of hanging tape with the mop so that it is above the hole, and bang at it until it sticks, leaving the new tile secured over the cavity, rather like a flap.

This will of course take a little practice. If the tape does not stick first time and you find the tile hurtling towards you down the slope, put something over your teeth.

Relocating the TV Aerial for Spring Using Only Curtain-rails and a Brick

High winter winds can play havoc with a roof aerial, which may be either VHF or UHF, depending on how much you know about it.

If you start getting flat heads and little legs, there is no need to bother either with expensive know-alls from the Yellow Pages or dangerous ladders. A TV aerial can be turned quite easily from inside the house by attaching an ordinary brick to a fifteen-foot length of metal curtain-rail with a stout rubber band or surgical tape, both available from the normal stockists. Simply choose the window nearest to the chimney holding the aerial, open it, and feed the curtain-rail out, brick-first.

Stand an assistant in the garden who will direct your aim. He should also be able to see a television screen by looking through the window, and wear a tin hat, or, if that is not to hand, a heavy-duty basin. Since the weight of the brick may cause the curtain-rail to wobble a bit, have a few practice runs before committing yourself to the stroke, then, when ready, simply swing the rail upward in the direction of the aerial. The brick will strike the aerial, knocking it into a different position. Eventually, on an agreed signal from your assistant, you will hit on the correct position for perfect pictures, provided the brick does not come off.

Keep the curtain-rail by you. Later in the year, with a sharp meat axe firmly bound to the (far) end, it will be indispensable for pruning remoter twigs . . .

. . . Or for Getting Tennis Balls out of Guttering

All pitched roofs are designed to allow tennis balls to roll down them at a speed carefully calculated to ensure that they lodge in a gutter. Quite why this should be cannot be explained except by pointing out that building is a masonic pursuit, and that people prepared to roll up one trouser-leg and throw blancmange at each other should not perhaps be let out during daylight hours.

In any event, spring is a time for going up the ladder with

our invaluable curtain-rail and using it to poke the tennis ball out of the guttering. Since all tennis balls are always seventeen feet away from where you thought they were when you looked out of the attic window, this invariably means that you will find yourself laying the curtain-rail inside the gutter, pushing it towards the tennis ball with the full extent of your arm, and giving it one final expertly desperate shove to ensure that (a) the ball flies out, and (b) the curtain-rail stays there, beyond reach.

The best way to get the curtain-rail out is to go down the ladder again and throw the tennis ball at the gutter in the hope that the retaining shackles are rusted enough to allow the gutter to fall away from the roof, bringing the curtain-rail down with it.

They generally are.

Removing a Damaged Chimney Pot without Spending £££s

This winter has been particularly hard on the standard terracotta chimney pot, for a variety of reasons. In many homes, the cold weather has persuaded people that there is nothing quite like a good old-fashioned fire, which has meant that even some expert handymen have occasionally got into trouble through refusing to be defrauded by ratfaced opportunist scum offering to clean chimneys, and preferring to do it themselves.

The method is quite simple. An ordinary household broom is fixed to half a hoe-handle, which in turn is stoutly roped to a length of flexible curtain-rail connected to an old mashie by any adhesive tape you happen to have left over from tiling. This is then fed up the chimney until the broom-head, being oblong, wedges in the chimney pot. A few sharp bangs should then bring all the soot down. This, however, may, upon close inspection, turn out to have a few terracotta shards in it, and the wise workman would be well advised to complete the job by knocking the chimney off.

Alternatively, damage can also result if, by sheer mis-chance, the attempt to improve BBC2 reception falls prey to a sudden treacherous gust, and the brick swings back with half a chimney following it. In this case, too, the meticulous expert will wish to remove the remains rather than, say, have birds fly into its sharp edges and roll dying into his downpipes. Where roofs are concerned, one must anticipate every eventuality.

How, though, is one to go about it? We have all listened to those so-called professionals who maintain there is nothing for it but to climb a ladder and set to work with a pick-axe, but those of us who have tried lashing out with a pick-axe tied to a curtain-rail know just how awkward that can be, especially when neighbours discover the exact nature of what is sticking out of their Volvo roof.

Nor, for the same reason, should one simply stand on the garage and shy rocks at the thing. One should stand on the garage and attempt to get a rope around it. Not, it must be stressed, a lasso, which, though undeniably romantic, lies beyond the expertise of even the keenest, but a simple strand of sashcord, thrown over the roof and caught by an assistant standing on the other side, i.e. in the road, who can then throw it back so that a loop is formed around the chimney. It is sensible to attach a brick to the thrown end of the rope to facilitate its flight, and it would thus be a wise precaution to cordon the road off briefly at each end, in case (a) the assistant misses the brick and it strikes a passing motorist or (b) the assistant attempts to catch the brick and is run over by a passing motorist. (*The best way to cordon a road off is to make little tripods, with any bits of hoe- and spade-handles you may have in your workshop, and stretch a length of curtain-rail between them.*)

Once the loop is in position, a sharp tug should bring the damaged chimney tumbling safely down the roof, dislodging no more than a few tiles which can be taped back into position, along with any guttering, downpipes, TV aerials, and so forth.

If a sharp tug is not sufficient to remove it, however, your wisest course would be to relocate the rope ends so that they hang down on the road side of the house, attach them to your rear bumper, and drive off slowly.

You will now discover the wisdom of not using the pick-axe. With luck, your neighbour will be prepared to run you to the station in the Volvo, until your car is back from the body-shop.

Summer Aid

HALLO, READERS, everywhere!

Or possibly chums.

Playmates, even.

Accurate flavour is of the essence, when one is charged with rolling back the arches of the years. Ask anyone. The spectrum of arcane nostalgic sensibilia has to be sidled up on with meticulous precision, if only to avoid over-writing.

I bring you yestersummer.

That unique searing agony of a sunburnt thigh meeting the leather of a Riley Monaco left broiling beneath the Clacton sun! The poignant clunk of a tiny truncheon thwacking the skull of Mrs Punch, the quite unforgettable scent of a duff winkle shimmering evilly upon its pin, the bizarre crackle of a thumb unintentionally involved in notching a deckchair! The heart-stopping glimpse of one's first fine extra-familial buttock, as a frisky gust snapped at the towel of a wriggling disrober, the chilling shock when a casual glance at one's toffee-apple discovered half a wasp still stuck to the bitten rim, the clutch of an old inner-tube around one's chest and the puckering tang of the oil-rainbowed sea as the wake of the *Skylark* dragged one down!

Don't talk to me about the plangency of dunked madeleines: if Proust had spent a childhood day at Southend-on-Sea, he'd be churning out the resonant verbiage yet. We could be looking at the wrong end of sixty vols.

Is it mere estival nostalgia that persuades me to lay out my stall today? It is not. Even while you sleep, and so far unannounced, I have snatched up a patriotic challenge which stands poised to touch us all.

I have been charged with restoring the English Summer.

It is a great and moving commission. Ensconced atop Ten Downing Street last week in the private apartments thrillingly refurbished to replicate the set of *This Happy Breed* and tucking in to a gourmet snack of fishcakes and Bev, I listened rapt while my hostess outlined another of her stunning reconstructional plans for her country. Her voice was low – one could hear, beyond the muslinned windows, the sound of Richard Branson picking up lolly sticks – as she explained how *terribly* important it was to return to those values which once bespoke England's greatness and which, rekindled, should, in less time that it takes to tell, make it great again.

The interview was characteristically short and to the point. Had my father ever owned a Morris Eight? Did my mother keep Williams Bros tokens in an empty Radio Malt jar? Could I whistle anything by Troyes and his Mandoliers? What did Old Hethers drink? Did either of my grandfathers wear a Linia belt? What was Sharp's the word for?

Within ten minutes, the Prime Minister had made her decision.

I have carte blanche. I have a generous budget carved from the television rights of *Kane and Abel*. I have a draftee workforce of up to 3,432,161 volunteers eager to do their bit for the nation that made them available.

I have a few preliminary ideas.

ICE-CREAM

It is a well-known fact that a country's moral decline may be measured in direct ratio to the complexity of what it licks. Show me a nation that gobbles things called Emperor Cherrynutola Daiquiriflakes, which come in long tin-foil tubes with a plastic spoon bolted to one side, a lewd endorsement from Roland Rat gummed to the other, and a Lucky Scratch'n'Win Lid which offers a free trip on Concorde to meet the Orient Express, and I will show you a nation poised on the rim of oblivion.

I have thus initiated a return to the Good Honest Wafer. The GHW – as millions of you will mistily recall – is a simple treat consisting of a small brick of semi-chilled lard loosely sandwiched between two oblongs of pre-saturated cardboard. It comes not in kiwi, mango, lychee or kumquat, but in vanilla only. You send a child to buy three of these with a dodecagonal coin, and when the child comes back with a slimy elbow and a fistful of pulp, you smack the child's head smartly, since intrafamilial authority is what will make this country great again.

Summer Aid has commissioned six thousand of this country's workshy to build several million GHWs on the Eldorado Trading Estate, Didcot, from which they will be despatched nationwide and sold by men with straw hats, striped aprons, waxed moustaches, and filthy hands. A little botulism never hurt anyone.

CRICKET

The summer game being not merely a national sport but also a national metaphor, the Prime Minister and I feel that draconian measures are necessary if inevitability is to be removed from the day when England goes down by an innings to a Liechtenstein Mixed Infants XI.

We have both had quite enough of designer pansies turning out in Chobham Armour to face dusky spinners and sniffing the contents of their hollowed bat-handles between such overs as they manage to survive. At the Summer Aid O My Hornby And My Barlow Long Ago Centre, thickset knotty men generously released from uneconomic pits and chosen for their cropped hair, broken noses, Popeye forearms, blue chins, narrow eyes and filthy tempers will be drilled by aristocratic martinets in the art of short-pitched bowling to a legside trap, and trained to go down the wicket to hit seamers on the half-volley. Their only protection will be an England cap, rolled up inside their underpants, and a dab of Brylcreem to ensure that any ball striking the head will skid away from close fielders. They will receive twelve pounds per week, plus a half-crown bonus for every manslaughter charge.

THE OPEN ROAD

Can anything more sharply evoke the memory of imperial greatness than the rolling English road, eight feet wide at its blind corners, a cow standing in the middle of it, an octogenarian midwife overtaking the cow on her asymmetrical Rudge, and the throaty noise of an old MG falling to bits as the undergraduate owner, attempting to avoid these hazards, unwisely applies his dated brakes?

There is no need whatever for these poignant features to have disappeared. We at Summer Aid have been looking into it, and we have discovered the necessary components to be in greater supply than ever.

Thanks to farsighted planning by our great Ministry of Transport, the hated, dehumanizing and nauseatingly foreign system of motorways is virtually at an end. A patriotic combination of dingbat design, unanticipated subsidence, shrewd mismanagement, tinpot engineering, acid drizzle, and fourteen million orange cones has ensured that Britain now has no straight wide boring roads at all, but several thousand delightful miles of winding contraflow, not a whit distinguishable from the stuff down which Dornford Yates would slide in third.

Given that our farmers are, at the same time, more preoccupied with planting rape and reaping subsidies than sitting with an unprofitable teat in each hand, it will come only as an immense relief to them to know that, even as I write, four whole Jobcentresful of Summer Aid draftees are going around the queendom, opening gates and releasing cows up slip roads; while, with the simultaneous streamlining of the NHS under its zesty new regional administrators, whole regiments of disbanded nurses are pedalling the landscape looking for ad hoc private deliveries in areas not covered by the public sector, i.e. beyond a three-mile radius of Oxford Circus.

Open tourers will be furnished by British Leyland by the simple expedient of shaking a BL saloon until the roof falls off. Undergraduate drivers are, of course, ten a penny, this being the likely saving to the nation of university cuts. Any undergraduates left over after the tourers are filled will be dressed in khaki jodhpurs and given old Norton sidecar combinations in which they will sit at junctions and salute all motorists sporting an original non-plastic AA badge. Any AA man attempting to abuse his position by selling annuities, Barry Manilow socket sets, cases of Reader's Digest tinned plums, or holidays on the Polish Riviera, will be shot on sight by the Stonehenge constabulary.

BEACHES

First, of course, the appalling drift towards nudity will cease forthwith. At this very moment, thousands of happy ex-jobfree knitters are cheerily beavering away at reproduction woollen bathing-costumes (*please state whether burgundy or navy when ordering*) complete with undetachable unigender vest and guaranteed to sag to mid-thigh, thereby reducing the risk of sexual identification at a stroke.

It has further come to our attention that the smell of the English strand has undergone a fearful deterioration since 1949, its last decent year. Where once a heady aroma of Nivea, milk stout, Anzora, sweat, pilchard and Zambuk held sway, decent beachgoers now find themselves contaminated with a foul aura composed mainly of trashy foreign designer unguents and take-away moussaka. Henceforth, all British beaches will be patrolled by offshore volunteer inflatables charged with the detergent hosing of anything not available in 1948 Grantham.

THE COUNTRYSIDE

There is little amiss with the summer countryside that cannot be remedied through sensitive patrolling by volunteers with baseball bats. Most hippies, foreign tourists, anti-nuclear perverts, rambling vegans, progressive vicars, weekending executive adulterers and the like will respond to a hearty swat, leaving the way clear for OAP volunteers on seasonal Summer Aid loan from inner-city mugging wards to hobble about in borrowed Panama hats and seersucker suits, selling jams and jellies, solving tricky aristocratic murders, and generally evoking all that was best about the inter-war years.

Not that urban and industrial Britons should be excluded from our green and pleasant shires. Summer Aid does not intend to put them all on to small allotments in their braces; many will be encouraged to join our works outings, where they will be driven about in vintage AEC charabancs with crates of screw-top Mackeson's roped to the roof, and encouraged to form widdling lines along hedgerows special-ly selected for their resilience. They will, of course, be firmly discouraged from singing *Viva España!* in favour of *Any Old Iron*.

All members will be issued with a free knotted hand-kerchief, a dish of jellied eels, five Woodbines, and a copy of *Reynolds News*.

One important point: should any such works outing find itself disembarked upon a rural riverbank in order to, say, do the Hokey-Cokey, and should they then find floating past them puntloads of gangling Summer Aid volunteers in blond wigs and false projecting teeth, they will immediately throw their knotted handkerchiefs in the air and cry 'God bless you, Guv'nor!' or similar.

The reason for this is simply that, with an election only four years away, it may very well prove electorally necessary for our great leader to declare war; and, caring person that she so manifestly is, she is absolutely determined that everyone, irrespective of rank, should be offered a poignant memory of That Last Golden Summer Before The Storm Clouds Gathered.

I've Got You Under My Skin

A vast hoard of long-lost songs and scores from old Broadway musicals has been discovered in a Warner Brothers vault in New York.

The collection includes hundreds of manuscripts by composers from Broadway's golden age: Gershwin, Herbert, Kern, Rodgers, Porter.

'The Cole Porter material alone could be worth millions,' said one copyright lawyer who for the past five years has devoted himself to nothing else, 'if the right collector came along.'

New York Times

AS THE pale moon rose above Manhattan, Sam Goldfarb eased himself out from behind his littered desk, sighed, trudged wearily through the deep and silent pile, and laid his furrowed forehead against the cooling glass.

Fifty-nine floors below, headlights twinkled along Seventh Avenue.

'In the still of the night,' he murmured softly, 'as I gaze from my window . . .'

His assistant, wrestling at the further desk with a complex bid from the Teamsters' Pension Fund for *Begin the Beguine*, glanced up. Goldfarb did not turn. He stared at the roster etched upon the window – Dexter, Weinrib, Weinrib, Simcox, Hayes, Goldfarb & Dexter, Attorneys-at-Law – and sighed once more.

'Have you heard, among this clan,' he said, 'I am called the Forgotten Man?'

'Well, did you ever?' said Kowalski, and dropped his head again to his documents.

Five years, thought Goldfarb. We've all been at this too long. I'm sixty-two. What am I doing five hundred feet up in an air-conditioned box, trying to play J. Paul Getty off against the V & A?

'Give me land, lots of land, under starry skies above,' he muttered, 'don't fence me in.'

'I happen to like New York,' said Kowalski, punching his keyboard. 'I happen to like this town. I like the city air, I like to drink of it, the more I know New York, the more I think of it.'

Goldfarb snorted, and crossed the room to lean over Kowalski's VDU.

'*I* want to ride to the ridge where the West commences,' he snapped, 'and gaze at the moon till I lose my senses!'

Kowalski, shrewdly sensing the crux towards which the five claustrophobic years had so frequently nudged them, now resignedly pushed his keyboard aside in search of compromise, and smiled up.

'I love Paris,' he said, finally.

'In the summer,' said Goldfarb, nodding, 'when it sizzles.'

'I love Paris in the winter,' corrected Kowalski.

Goldfarb stared at him.

'When it *drizzles*?' he cried incredulously.

Kowalski shrugged, and bent again to his contractual duties.

Their secretary shimmered in with coffee and sandwiches. Goldfarb's fatigue-addled eyes watched from behind the teetering piles of yellowed scores as the unfettered bust trembled towards him, looked away when, as she set down his little tray, the decolletage yawned.

'In olden days,' he observed, when the door had closed behind her, 'a glimpse of stocking was looked on as something shocking.'

'According to the Kinsey Report,' said Kowalski, 'every average man, you know, much prefers to . . .'

Goldfarb spat coffee.

'Too darn hot?' enquired Kowalski, solicitously.

Goldfarb shook his head.

'You do something to me!' he shouted. 'Something that simply mystifies me. Tell me, why should it be, you . . .'

126

But Kowalski was no longer listening. Having bitten into his triple-decker, his mouth now puckered like a walnut, and pausing only to evacuate it into a Kleenex, he flung open the door into the outer office, and, waving the remains of the sandwich, shrieked:

'What is that thing *called*, love?'

He came back slowly into the room, glanced at Goldfarb's glum face, sighed, softened, opened the small personal fridge that lay concealed behind a row of half-morocco dummy lawbook-spines, took out a bottle, and showed the label to his morose superior.

'Little one?' said Kowalski.

'I was so gloomy?' enquired Goldfarb.

Kowalski nodded. He thumbed, and the cork flew.

'This French champagne,' he said. 'So good for the brain!'

Goldfarb shook his head.

'I get no kick from champagne,' he explained. 'Mere alcohol doesn't thrill me at all.'

The younger man looked at him for a moment or two, considering carefully.

'Who wants to wallow in champagne?' he murmured. He put down the bottle, crossed to his desk, opened a drawer, and paused.

'Some get a kick from cocaine,' he said.

Goldfarb raised his hands in horror.

'I know that if I took only one sniff . . .'

'Get out of town?'

Goldfarb nodded.

'Before it's too late,' he said.

Kowalski pursed his lips. Old guys, what could you do with them? Still, why waste an unlocked drawer? He took out his silver box and opened it, under Goldfarb's uneasy glare.

'In Spain, the best upper sets do it,' explained Kowalski.

'Lithuanians and Letts do it?' enquired Goldfarb sarcastically.

'Not to mention the Finns,' nodded Kowalski.

Goldfarb looked away. Young guys, what could you do with them?

'Why should I care?' he said to himself. 'Why should I cry?'

He would have preferred 'I should care?', of course; but it wasn't his to sing.

The telephone on Kowalski's desk jangled. Kowalski, who had sunk into a deep and dreamful sleep, lurched awake to find Goldfarb rummaging in a heap of yellowing lyrics for the buried receiver.

'What's this awful hullaballoo?' cried Kowalski. 'What's this awful hullabaloo? Who are you and who are you, what's this awful hullabaloo?'

'It was just one of those things,' snapped Goldfarb sarcastically. 'One of those bells that now and then rings!'

He found the instrument, and snatched it up. His eyes widened. His hand slid over the mouthpiece.

'It's the top!' he gasped.

'It's the Coliseum?' whispered Kowalski.

Goldfarb rolled exasperated eyes.

'It's the *top*!' he cried.

Kowalski's mouth fell open.

'It's the Louvre Museum?'

Goldfarb nodded, and reached out, flailing wildly. Kowalski thrust his calculator into his master's groping hand, his own trembling: who knew, maybe it was the Big One? Maybe they would dig deep.

Maybe they would buy the whole lousy lot.

Kowalski chewed his lip, and watched Goldfarb's face. In answer, Goldfarb covered the mouthpiece again.

'It only happens in dreams!' he whispered. He jabbed the calculator buttons. He jotted on this pad, and on that. Eventually he shouted into the phone: 'C'est magnifique!' and banged it joyously down.

He grasped Kowalski's forearm, and his eyes shone.

'Wunderbar!' he roared.

'Wunderbar?'

Goldfarb fell back and steadied himself against the panelling.

'Yes,' he croaked, 'it's truly wunderbar!'

Kowalski burst into tears. They were free!

Kowalski threw his arms around Goldfarb, and kissed him.

Goldfarb drew back, and looked at his young assistant.

Kowalski blushed.

'While tearing off a game of golf,' he murmured, 'I may make a play for the caddy.'

Goldfarb crossed slowly to his own desk, and sat down.

'It's the wrong time?' asked Kowalski. 'And the wrong place?'

Goldfarb looked at Kowalski, though not unkindly, and shook his head. After a moment or two, Kowalski blew his nose.

'It's the wrong game?' he enquired.

'With the wrong chips,' said Goldfarb.

Strings Attached

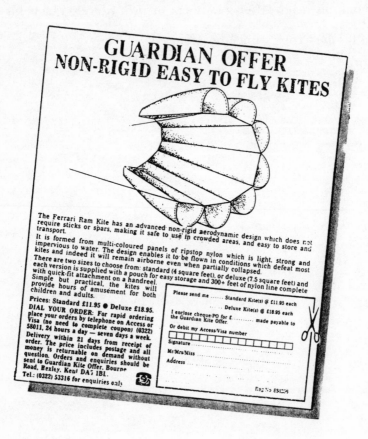

To the Editor of the Guardian

Sir,–It is difficult to know where to begin.

I speak not only as a loyal reader of many years standing, but as one who has also, through that selfsame loyalty, availed himself over those years of many of your Special Offers, frequently at great personal cost, e.g. jogging in my Snug Brushed-Cotton Track Suit With Smart Guardian Logo Prominently Displayed and having half-bricks thrown at me by Nazi skinheads to cries of *Nobody loves a fairy when she's forty!* and similar – not that it is their fault, I blame the iniquitous tabloid propaganda of their Wapping sturmbannführers, combined, of course, with council house mildew, junkfood additives, ambient nicotine, chemical lager, and so forth, we are all of us

130

responsible are we not? – also getting backache something terrible while reclining in my Guardian Woven Willow Furniture, I have been meaning to write to you about that for years, I am not wholly convinced it was personally woven by boat people and if it was not I do not see why I should have to put up with walking around all day bent double.

Especially as I thus present so much slower a target to under-privileged *Sun* youngpersons that I have taken to wearing a Guardian Special Offer Stainless Steel Saucepan on my head. Its inside may well invite certain vegan items to bond themselves permanently to it, but its outside is splendidly sturdy, it will take anything up to a paving-stone with hardly a dent, a feature to be borne in mind when one is simul-taneously shod in Guardian Discount Hiking Boots and can accelerate only by removing them and hanging them around one's neck, where their weight tends, at speed, to leave ugly weals on the clavicle.

However, with your latest offer, everything has changed. In all my long association with your newspaper, I have never been so shocked.

Can I be the only *Guardian* reader worrying what a kite might do to a Heavyside Layer already at such horrifying risk from the deadly effluvia of billions of homicidal cigarettes, vehicle exhausts, nuclear tests, stuff coming up from murdered foxes, satellite invasion, non-vegetarian methane exhalations of one kind and another, South Africa, polysaturated margarine fall-out, shotgun pellets, and that stuff some people spray under their arms in order to deny their humanity?

A kite might just be the straw that breaks the camel's back. A standard 4 square feet hole in the ionosphere does not bear thinking about, let alone a de luxe 7.5 square feet one. I am no scientist, Sir, but do not tell me that it is beyond the bounds of possibility for the moon to fall through it or something. It would make Chernobyl look like a vicarage tea party. I note that you supply 300+ feet of nylon line, but that no mention is made of exactly what that +

stands for. I think we should be told.
Artemus Sims,
Balliol

Sir,–Hum! A pussonal assistant just wippin in f'om de Council sauna an' informin' me where she seen a refrence to MULTI-COLOURED PANELS in your obbernoxious rag. It plain as de nose on a pikestaff where dis is a obvious malicious swipe at de elected reppersentatives of dis proud burrow. You off de libry shelfs forthwith, plus fish shops, municipal khazis, an' ole age honkies' sheltered beddin'.
Paramount Cllr Bernie Monolulu,
Haringey

Sir,–Can I believe my eyes? Has the callous and uncaring term 'non-rigid' actually appeared in the *Guardian?*

I trust, Sir, I do not have to draw pictures, we are all persons of the world and a nod is as good as a wink to a blind horse; although both, of course, may cause offence in the workplace, and one would be well advised to seek a ruling. Nods and winks, that is, not blind horses; although, naturally, I should have no objection to a blind horse in the workplace, being myself a committed equal opportunities employer, presently in hand-crocheted non-animal moccasins, where there is not, admittedly, a lot of work for a blind horse, but this isn't to say that if work came up suitable for a blind horse, e.g. pulling a home-made wooden cart laden with organic moccasin material along, say, non-ferrous rails, we should not be more than happy to employ it – pursuant, of course, to the stipulations of our Horse Rights colleagues, and with a strict incumbency upon our other employees not to make horsist jokes should it inadvertently stumble into something, say, or leave a doings anywhere.

Let me simply point out that many of your readers will experience non-rigidity situations from time to time. Or even more frequently, if they happen to have contracted – to choose a random example – a mysterious form of NSU brought on, in the opinion of most leading homeopaths, by fumes generated when banyan leaves are boiled to make moccasins. Many of these people have learned to overcome their periodic non-rigidity and lead fulfilling lives, and by not only drawing attention to their little shortcoming but also suggesting that, if one does not have the good fortune to be a kite, one is required to correct the situation with, and I quote, 'sticks or spars', you expose the non-rigid to an uninformed derision which is the hallmark of the beast.

Need I add that there is much more to being a quote man unquote than holding a primitive colonial threat over some unlucky woman?
Jolyon Elgar, Hon Sec,
L.I.M.P.
Barnes

Sir,–Millions of us have been sickened to the deepest core of our being by the line **Mr/Mrs/Miss** in what you no doubt gleefully refer to as your box. Is it just possible that something could be missing from this gut-crunching collection of neo-Tsarist labels?

And what, precisely, is 'ripstop nylon', you drooling fascist bastard?
Ms Malvolia Greenham,
Holyrood House

Sir,–What your readership will make of the phrase 'even when partially collapsed', we dare not begin to think. It suggests there is something wrong with being partially collapsed. At a time when many of us are campaigning to persuade restaurants, discos, public libraries, slipper baths, USAF perimeter fences, and so forth, to make proper provision for the partially collapsed victims of the Thatcherite holocaust, your heartless and insensitive language threatens to set back our cause by hundreds, perhaps thousands, of years.
Jeffrey Bernard,
Michael ffolkes,
Peter Langan,
Waterloo Bridge

Sir,–I have just noticed the advertisement placed in your paper by the Ferrari Ram Kite. Unless I am very much mistaken, this is the same thieving bastard who took £700 off me in 1969 in return for a bus-ticket to Kathmandu to join his, what was it, Ashcan, where I was led to believe I would be met by a big sloe-eyed number with an emerald in her navel who would instruct me in the meaning of life, e.g. Lecture One: Why Are We All Here?, Lecture Two: Where Are We All Going?, Lecture Three: What Is It All For?, and so on for a fortnight until I attained Havana, I think it was, anyway it would all be peace and light and you could grow your own stuff without the old bill coming round and saying go on you little bastard tell me it's marigolds. I was also given to understand it was endorsed by a major Beatle.

In the event, the coach broke a half-shaft outside Sevenoaks and totalled a gravel-bin and the Kent filth asked to see the driver's insurance and we all ended up legging it across this ploughed field and when I tried to locate the Ferrari Ram Kite at the address on his letter-head, it turned out to be over a tattoo parlour and he had done a runner owing three months rent plus two instalments on a red parrot with Hare Krishna coming out of its beak on his left wossname.

For your information, the Ferrari Ram Kite is a tall bony bugger with a straggly beard, also got half a parrot going Har on his bum unless he's conned some other mug for the balance, and if he turns up to collect any of his £11.95 cheques, you would be doing a great favour if you tipped the wink to
Eamonn Menuhin RN,
H.M.S. Mollusc

132

Sir,–My little Scottish friend tells me you
are selling T-shirts with NON-RIGID
EASY TO FLY KITES written on them.
Since he rarely gets things wrong, could
we have two, please? I enclose his
cheque for £23.90.
David Owen,
Limehouse

PS You may of course feel that, as this
succinct slogan snappily encapsulates not
only our electoral policy but also your
editorial one, you would prefer to waive
payment in this case.

April's Shower

'GOOD MORNING, Inspector!'

'Good morning, Sir Dennis! And, as your loyal and devoted Tax Inspector, may I be the first to congratulate you upon the splendid part you played in the Guinness Affair?'

'But I played no part in the Guinness Affair, Inspector.'

'It is that upon which I congratulate you, Sir Dennis!'

'Ha, ha, ha!'

'Ha, ha, ha!'

'Well met, Inspector! What a good one! Do have a cigar.'

'Oh, I say, I really couldn't. I don't somehow feel –'

'Nonsense, old man! Celebrate the end of the tax year. Courtesy of the Sir Dennis Plumrose Cigar Distribution Company.'

'That's a – thank you so much – that's a new one on me. You didn't have it this time last year, did you?'

'Quite. Set it up on April 6. Little non-profit-making concern of mine. Registered charity, of course. Supported with funds from other Plumrose companies, donations to buy cigars for cigarless unfortunates.'

'I see. Rather like your Bubbly Aid '85, I take it?'

'Similar. Slightly smaller print, ha, ha, ha! It's all there on page eighty-seven of my tax return.'

'Odd, I don't remember noticing –'

'Listed under Ferrari, old chap.'

'Ferrari?'

'Exactly. Charity-worker for the use of. Need it to drive around the various companies, collecting donations. It's cross-referenced under Yacht, Steam, Bigger One, by the way. Being the registered office of the Fund.'

'Ah, yes, here we are, quite so. It's moored at Antibes, I see.'

'My wife's chest.'

'I'm sorry?'

'Bronchitis. Plays her up terribly. Has to spend half the year on the Riviera. Frightfully sad. And as she's the cigar company treasurer, there was no other course.'

'I quite understand. That would account for those forty-one business trips on your part?'

'Spot on, old man. And the Plumrose Convalescent Home running expenses, of course.'

'Ah, yes. I see that there are now four of these sanatoria listed. Gstaad, Mayfair and Barbados. As well as Antibes.'

'That's it. Least I could do, really. Can't have the directors succumbing to the fearful stresses of executive life, can we, Inspector? You must have read about them. All over the place. Can't open a newspaper.'

'And this paediatric clinic?'

'Excuse me?'

'The one that appears to occupy the entire top floor of the Savoy.'

'Ah. That one. Yes. That's for my son Nigel. Director of eighteen subsidiary companies of Plumrose Holdings plc.'

'He's three, I believe?'

'Coming up to four, actually. An awful worrier. Needs full-time attention when he's thinking about production hiccups, union demands, strength of the yen, all that kind of thing. Hence the Plumrose Savoy Clinic and Child Care Centre. And, of course, the nursing expenses.'

'His mother?'

'Precisely! Wonderful woman. Prepared to drop everything in Antibes or Gstaad and fly in at a moment's notice if the boy needs her. That's why Plumrose Engineering (Grand Cayman) Inc bought her the Rolls.'

'In grateful appreciation?'

'Nail on the head, Inspector, ha, ha, ha! There's not much gets past you! My son's a project consultant there, you see.'

'I do indeed, Sir Dennis. By the way, Plumrose Engineering seems to have spent a considerable amount on sable during this tax year, doesn't it?'

'One of the saddest industrial stories of 1986, Inspector. Grandchildren yet unborn will weep and tremble at the tale. What happened was, Plumrose Engineering's experimental division bought these twelve sable coats –'

'For two hundred thousand pounds.'

'– for two hundred thousand pounds, for the purpose of testing the experimental Plumrose Automatic Self-Folding Chinchilla Coat-hanger.'

'Which failed?'

'Dismally. Terrible loss. Had to give all the coats away.'

'You couldn't have sold them, I suppose?'

'Shame on you, old man! Haven't got a licence to trade in furs, have I? Haven't got any retail outlets. My word, you'd have been down on that like a ton of thingies! No flies on you chaps, eh?'

'Thank you, Sir Dennis. They seem to have been given to your osteopaths.'

'I'm sorry?'

'The chinchillas. You've listed these twelve osteopathic masseuses, where are we, Doctor Mandy Stilletto, Matron Siun Sha Irrigami, Fraulein-Scoutmistress Ilse –'

'Ah, yes. Absolutely. Yes, in my capacity as chairman of Plumrose Offshore Hypermarkets, I decided to give the company doctors their Christmas bonuses in kind. Faithful servants, Inspector, faithful servants, one must look after them. They are thin on the ground.'

'How uncomfortable for you.'

'What?'

'No matter. Just my little joke. Incidentally, I note that their twelve company flats have all been redecorated again.'

'Naturally. Nothing worse than a dowdy osteopath. They need the colour TVs for their work, by the way. Research into spinal discomfort brought about by watching TV in bed.'

'Ah. I must say I'm somewhat surprised by the loss incurred when Plumrose Tubing Ltd, the Plumrose Brick Company and Plumrose Chiming Horseblankets were sold. I'd expected a nice little capital gain for you there. As well as for us, ha, ha, ha!'

'Nothing I'd have liked better, old chap. But, unfortunately, that's the way things go sometimes.'

'What is?'

'I'm afraid I had to sell those three companies to my daughter. She's always had her eye on them. And how can one make a profit out of one's own flesh and blood?'

'She appears to have paid £2.83 for the lot, Sir Dennis.'

'All there was in her piggy-bank, Inspector. I let her keep the shirt button and Teddy's eye. Tough I may be, but unfeeling, never.'

'Very decent of you.'

'Well, she likes to bite on them, and I couldn't in all conscience –'

'Teething?'

'Right first time. Which also explains the family's –'

'Dental trip to the Bahamas. I quite understand.'

'Knew you would.'

'I see Mr F. Scott Perelman Jr of Orange, New Jersey, is still living with you?'

'Our foreign customer, yes. It's his second year of residence at Plumrose Convalescent Towers.'

'Has he placed any orders for Plumrose products yet?'

'He's still thinking about it, Inspector. Still being, as it were, wooed.'

'He appears to have an enormous appetite. Not to say expensive. Not to say discriminating.'

'It was the three hundredweight of foie gras you were thinking of, no doubt?'

'And the ten gross of Dom Perignon.'

'Often gets up in the night, Inspector. Often pops downstairs for a quick stone or two of caviar and a couple of crates of Château Petrus '61. Just between you and me, he's a bit of a pig.'

'Couldn't throw him out, though?'

'Unthinkable. Shocking bad manners. Besides, think of all those American orders we might get. One day, who knows, big bucks for you, peerage for me, sky's the limit under this Government, eh?'

'In my own humble experience, Sir Dennis, business enterprise has never been more vigorous.'

'Chap's a wordsmith! You're in the wrong profession, Inspector! Happy New Tax Year!'

'Happy New Tax Year, Sir Dennis.'

Party Games

At home, challenger Anatoly Karpov, despite his dedication, is an eager socialite, almost as keen on the cocktail party circuit as on the chess circuit.

Today

K.U. CHERNENKO FATHER'S DAY RECEPTION
HALL OF SPANNERS   19/1/1985

White: A. Karpov   Black:Sonya Alulyeva
Dropped Peanut Gambit Declined
Rick's Bar Variation Opening (CAPABLANCA)

Karpov having dropped the peanut down the front of Sonya Alulyeva's smart hessian frock and received the conventional curled lip response, then deployed his favourite opening from Capablanca:

White: Of all the Halls of Spanners in all the world, you had to walk into mine.
Black: Why are you wearing a warehouse coat?
White: Nice try, Blue Eyes! This just happens to be the newest number in the GUM lightweight nearly-white tuxedo range, patch pocket, drape, genuine leatherette elbows, hood, don't tell me an elegant dame like you don't recognize it! How about coming back to my place and watching my bow spin?
Black: Saucebox!

Three standard moves ensued, and the position following Karpov's 'Here's looking at you, kid' was that Alulyeva found herself forked.

ANDREI GROMYKO COME-AS-YOU-ARE PARTY
HOTEL DE GEARBOX   23/5/85

White: A. Karpov   Black: G. R. Mishinsky
Polish Feint Opening followed by German Trap

Karpov, encountering an old cocktail circuit rival, lost no time in initiating a cunningly disguised frontal assault directly aimed at his opponent's most vulnerable point. Each having begun with a fairly friendly canapé exchange – Karpov took Mishinsky's stuffed olive, and Mishinsky replied by removing Karpov's twiglet – Karpov then moved very quickly to lull Mishinsky's notoriously suspect Lumpenproletariat Defence:

White: Still driving that old Lada, then?
Black: It takes me there and brings me back.
White: Really? Tell me, why does it take thirty-seven Poles to assemble a Lada?
Black: Big joke. What about you, smart arse, still got that clapped out Zim minivan?
White: Ha! I thought you'd never ask. It so happens I just took delivery of a Mercedes 450SEL, full air-conditioning, electric hood, ABS brakes, white pigskin upholstery with blue piping, Blaupunkt self-seeking radio, naturally with quadraphonic ...

Mishinsky resigned.

WELCOME COMRADE SCARGILL JAM TEA
SS20 BRASSERIE   8/9/1985

White: A.Karpov   Black: Sonya Alulyeva
A fascinating example of an attempted Dual Avoidance by White, producing from Black an unsettling Queen's Threat somewhat feebly countered by White with the old-fashioned English Defence.

It is generally agreed by commentators that Karpov came to this encounter ill-prepared. He was keenly expecting to play the Roman Decoy against Nikita Oblonowitz, the elderly Restaurant Grand Master, by casually enquiring whether he had ever eaten at the fashionable Ravioli-U-Like in Sverdlovsk (a restaurant which Karpov had just made up), but, upon turning from the vodka tray, he found himself instead to be looking straight at the lovely Sonya Alulyeva.

White: Oh. Look, I'm awfully sorry, I've got to go and, er.
Black: Have you told her yet?
White: I'm sorry?
Black: I said, have you told her yet?
White: Ah. The thing is, the thing is, she hasn't been feeling very well lately.

Unfortunately, Karpov's English Defence proved totally inadequate against Alulyeva's surprise next move, an Indian Attack Variation. This differs from the conventional move introduced by Valentine Green in the London Tournament of 1862 shortly after his return from India (1 e4 e5 2 d3), in that it is more a grasp of the front hair and an attempt to remove the scalp with a broken vodka carafe, and should perhaps more properly be designated an Injun Attack Variation, especially in view of the exceedingly good joke coined by G. R. Mishinsky, who happened to witness the move and made a lightning, albeit salacious, reference to Karpov's Last Stand.
  The match was abandoned.

POTEMKIN ANNIVERSARY TOMBOLA
BALLBEARING SUITE   14/11/85

White: A. Karpov   Black: G.R.Mishinsky
Remote Passed Pawn met by German Trap Reprise
Slav Revenge

Ever adroit at beguiling his opponent by an ostensibly respectful nod towards an earlier defeat and then turning the recalled tactics to his own ends, Mishinsky met Karpov's opening half-bow with an uncharacteristically boisterous clap

140

on the shoulder. Karpov's suspicions should have been aroused, but he had much on his mind: the cocktail circuit is a savage and mentally exhausting arena. Thus, Karpov's unguarded second move:

White: How's your good lady?
Black: Mustn't grumble. Course, she's no Sonya Alulyeva, nudge, nudge, catch my drift, no need to draw pictures, men of the world, eh?
White: For God's sake keep your voice down! That's her old man over there.
Black: Stone me, so it is! Doesn't he know about it, then?
White: About what?
Black: Nice car, the Lada.
White: What? Oh, yes, vastly underrated. You can't beat Polish technology. Streets ahead.
Black: Yes, they could teach the Krauts a thing or two about motor cars. How's that Merc of yours?
White: Rubbish! Junk! Always in the garage. Not fit for scrap.
Black: Dear, oh dear! What a silly sod you must feel!
White: Oh I do. All the time. Look, about the other thing –
Black: Other thing?
White: You wouldn't say anything to, er, thing. Alulyev?
Black: CHECK!
White: You bastard!

Fool's Mate.

RAITA GORBACHEV COCOA EVENING
SPARK PLUG ROOMS   18/12/1985

White: A.Karpov   Black: Sergei Mikhailovich Alulyev Lavatory Window Gambit Countered Sicilian Defence Deployed

A game beset with off-board intimidation. Several minutes passed before either player made an opening move, each eyeing the other silently until an intervention was made by the tournament organizer in the interest of time:

Hostess Gorbachev: Do you two know each other?
White: Er.

Black: I am Sergei Mikhailovich Alulyev.
White: Ah.
Black: You have been boffing my wife.
White: Er.
Black: Sonya Alulyeva.

After these six rapid but testingly unexpected moves, Karpov requested time out, and attempted to resign honourably by means of the Lavatory Window Gambit. Unhappily for the champion, the window proved to be locked. While he was attempting the Nailfile Opening, Alulyev appeared in the company of two men in Homburgs, and employed the Sicilian Defence:

Black: I would like you to meet Capo di Tutti Capi Zabaglione.
White: Er, welcome to the Spark Plugs Mens Room. I was just –
Black: And his chief torpedo, Enrico Fritti the Don.
White: No relation to the river, ha-ha-ha?
Black: Break his thumbs.

After Alulyev's brilliant fibula to rib 3, Karpov could do no more than improvise. He employed an unorthodox Knight's Resignation, which consists of two steps forward, one step sideways, and falling over.

Of Cabbages and Kings

'It's very important to talk to plants. They respond, I find.'
                                                    Prince Charles

RESPLENDENT IN his uniform of Colonel-in-Chief, the Queen's Own Herbaceous Borderers – an outfit he had, of course, and with his customary unerring flair, designed himself – he crunched slowly down the gravelled path, hands clasped, in their huge canvas ceremonial garden gloves, behind his back, dress gumboots buffed to an iridescent emerald, the gilt watercress of his epaulettes shimmering in the Highgrove sun, and inspected the serried ranks.

Halfway along the front row, he stopped, smiled a charming, if awkward smile, and tugged his earlobe. His straw busby wobbled slightly.

'Good morning,' he said.

A nervous tremor, which was only to be expected, rippled down the line. A throat cleared.

'Good morning, Your Royal Highness.'

The Prince's brow crinkled, as, from time to time, it will.

'Forgive me,' said the Prince, 'you are, er –'

'Sprout, sir.'

The Prince nodded.

'Ah. Sprout. Of course. Everything all right, Sprout?'

'Tickety-boo, sir. Hunky-dory. Top-hole.'

'Jolly good!' exclaimed the Prince. 'Splendid! That's the

stuff.' He glanced left, along the row. 'And what about you, Mr, er?'

Panic gripped the neighbour plant. Nothing came out but a hoarse and indecipherable croak.

'Begging your pardon, sir, but he is also called Sprout.'

'Is he?' cried the Prince. 'Is he really? How extraordinary!'

'We all are,' said the first sprout.

'What, everyone in this bed?' exclaimed the Prince. 'All one family?'

'There've been sprouts here for generations,' replied the sprout, proudly, 'sir.'

A bead of moisture softened the Prince's eye.

'A fine old Gloucestershire name, eh?' he murmured. He drew a handkerchief from the pocket of his scarlet smock, and blew his nose.

The sprout, in its turn, gave a discreet little cough.

'Begging your pardon, sir,' it said (it would later feel faint at the memory of its boldness), 'but we're Belgian originally. From what you might call Belgium. No disrespect, sir.'

The Prince, astonished, rocked back upon his rubber heels.

'Good heavens!' he cried. He thought for a moment or two. He tugged his earlobe furiously. He turned his signet ring. 'Plucky little Belgium, eh?' he offered, finally.

A bee thrummed past. A leaf fell, slowly. A far clock struck. The sprout could not be sure, but it thought it could feel itself growing.

'But we're all here now, sir,' it said, eventually. 'In England.'

'Yes,' said the Prince of Wales. 'Yes, so you are!'

He laughed.

They all laughed.

'Tell me,' said the Prince, taking the chased silver dibbling stick from beneath his arm and waving it about a bit, 'what exactly are you working on at the moment? As, er, as sprouts.'

The sprout, at last, sensing the ice breaking around it, relaxed a little.

'Growing,' it replied.

'Growing,' repeated the Prince, nodding. 'Aha, I see. That must be, er, that must involve, as it were –'

'We start small, and gradually we get bigger,' explained the sprout. 'Until we are big enough. Until we are, in the

144

technical parlance, grown.'

'Fascinating,' murmured the Prince, 'fascinating! Good Lord. Well I never. And no doubt, all this, er, all this growing that you have to do, required –' the huge blancoed gardening gloves made vague expressive circles in the air '– some kind of very special training?'

'Yes. Up sticks, mainly. For the first few months. They use this, what's the word?'

'Twine,' prompted a mutter from the row behind.

'Twine,' said the sprout.

'Twine, eh?' enquired the Prince, brow furrowed, lip chewed. 'Twine. My goodness. Twine.'

'In lay terms, Your Royal Highness,' explained the sprout, 'string.'

'Aha!' cried the Prince, nodding vigorously. 'Good old Johnny string! That accounts for a lot. I can see that. String.' He inclined slightly forward, peering at this sprout, and at that. 'And, training apart, I assume the job also requires some pretty tricky, er, professional skills?'

The neighbouring and hitherto tongue-tied sprout, suddenly emboldened by what it took to be the newly informal atmosphere, now spoke up.

'Definitely, Your Royal Highness, sir,' it cried. 'For a start, you would not credit the amount of photosynthesis involved!'

'You speak when you're spoken to,' muttered the first sprout.

'No, no!' cried the Prince. 'Do feel free. No pack drill. Woolly-pully order, eh?'

He laughed again.

And again, they all followed. One or two, indeed, became, uncharacteristically for sprouts, hysterical. Asides were murmured. Phews were phewed. He was a bit of a wag for a Royal Personage, all right, and no mistake, they did not care who knew it.

'This photo thing,' said the Prince, when they had all recovered somewhat, 'what exactly does it, um, involve?'

'Basically,' said the second sprout, 'and if Your Royal Highness will in his gracious almightiness forgive me for cutting a long story short, we take carbon dioxide and water out of the air, and convert them into carbohydrates by, well, not to put too fine a point on it, by exposing them to light.'

'Good heavens! It sounds jolly complicated. And yet

everyone manages to come out green.'

'Definitely, sir. It is something we, well, take pride in, in a manner of speaking. Though I says it as shouldn't.'

'Nonsense!' The Prince clasped his hands together, and spread them again, passionately. 'If only more people in this great country of ours took pride in what they . . .' he left the proposition eloquently unfinished, and turned, with the exquisite timing of his trade, to offer his attention to a smaller plant beside the path.

'And you, er, learned all this in Belgium?'

The plant said nothing.

After a long minute or two, the Prince tapped his dibbler against his gumboot.

'Is your colleague all right?' he enquired, perhaps a trifle testily. The day was unseasonally hot, he had twenty more beds to visit, a speech to make to the asparagus, a centenarian wisteria to honour, a new cold-frame to open, a blighted quince to comfort with Her Majesty's earnest good wishes.

'Begging Your Royal Highness's gracious pardon,' murmured the spout, 'he is a carrot.'

'A carrot? *A carrot?*'

'They interplant 'em,' explained the sprout.

The Prince stared at the tuft beside his welt.

'Is it deaf?' he enquired.

The sprouts hooted. The repeated query shuttlecocked back and forth across the rows. This would be something to tell their grandchildren. As it were. The day the Prince of Wales said *Is it deaf?*

'No, Your Highness, it is not deaf, it is working underground. You'd have to shout.'

'Underground? My goodness! Is this some kind of new, what's the word, process?'

'No, no, it is the traditional and time-honoured procedure with carrots. The red bit grows downwards, sir.'

'You mean –?'

But, despite the intensity with which the query was launched, despite the keen straining of the sprouts for the opportunity to make their responsive mark, it was, sadly, too late. The alarm upon his wrist tinkled. It was time to move on. In one single, practised, ineffably royal movement, the Prince stepped to a prepared plot, deftly planted a rutabaga, sprinkled a pinch of bonemeal from the bespoke little scabbard at his hip, tugged a drawstring to unveil a staked plaque testifying to his visit, saluted, waved, and left.

The third cheer echoed away among the massed vegetables.

'One,' said the first sprout, 'of nature's gentlemen.'

'Grace,' murmured his neighbour. 'Charm. Taste. *Style*.'

'He's much taller than I thought,' said a sprout from the second row.

'Did you notice how he put me at my ease?' said the first sprout.

'In my opinion,' called a sprout from the fourth row, 'his ears have been vastly exaggerated by the media.'

'And what a sense of humour!' cried the first sprout. 'That one about the deaf carrot!'

'He could go on the stage,' said the sprout from the second row.

'Charisma,' said the sprout beside him. 'That is the only word.'

A reflective silence fell.

Until the first sprout sighed, paused, and, at long last, spoke for them all.

'You'd never think the bastard was a vegetarian,' he said.

Oh Say, Can You See?

The great majority of American schoolchildren are distressingly incompetent when it comes to writing proficiently, according to a major Federal study. Most children were found to be unable to persuade, describe, or even imagine coherently. The study, by the National Assessment of Educational Progress, involved a test in which children were invited to write a persuasive letter to their imaginary Aunt May, asking her to allow the writer to visit her.

Daily Telegraph

7 arpil
dear aunt may,
i wuld like to come visit witchew. i am a good amercan kid i do not snif nothing and i do not shoot up and i do not screw around and i honor the flagg and i bleeve these untied states is one natoin under god and the rest is a bunch of dum forn barsteds.

i like rocky ivy and clit eastwards and god. the bit i like best about rocky ivy is wear he beets the shit out of this dum comnist and the bit i like best about clit eastwards is wear he says go on punk make mi day and bloes his hed off with this big .357 magnum he has and the bit i like best about god is wear he gets all the forners to walk into the see and then he shuts it and the sunsabitches all screem and go down the toobs and there is forn blood all over and this is how it gets to be the red see.

if you let me come visit witchew i wil look after you good. it is the amercan way to look after them who is less fortnate than us such as ole dames and all and stop them making dum assholes of themselfs. i wil walk witchew to cherch and the a & p and the d a r meatings and if any cheap nigre or mugra tries to get a hole of you i wil stik my fingras in his eys and do karaty on him.

rite me soon.

your nefew you aint met.

10 arpil

dear aunt may

maybe you dont heer too good.

i was figgrin to be visiting witchew by now. i packed my grip. i oiled my airgun. it is a dam good airgun. if you oil it good and keep it in shape the way they teech you at the littel christain rifle leegue you can shoot the ey out of any dago raper who culd be proulin aroun an ole dames hous.

also i tole the dawg we wuz going. i do not want to have to tel the dawg we aint goin he is one big dawg, he doan take kinely to having his plans changed by some crazy old broad. he is a gernam shepperd. he is traned to eat legs. he wuld be a good dawg for you an me to hav aroun the place in case some flaky loony-toon muslin came to the door and tried to stik us. i wuld just say kil him dook and that muslin wuld be lookin down at too stumps and wishin wear he had stayed in liberia.

i wuld not be no trubble i wuld just sit aroun the place scopin the a teem and miami vise and any videos you had wear they berned perverts alive until there fases shriveled off and you wuld feel good havin a spunky amercan kid on the premises. did i mentoin i also have a junior cubscout flak-jaket and a three-pound crucifix wear i have filed the edges down and put a lether thong on the end so it does not come off of your rist and you can keep on swingin even with three commie sluggs in you.

stil and all it is not the amercan way to go wear we aint wanted so the impotent thing is for you to rite me immediate and say deer nefew i luv amerca my hous is your hous come over anytime the icebox is full you wuld have your own room and color teevee and a big window with a ninety degree ark of fire.

i aim to give you the benfit of the dout aunt may. culd be you din get my letter on account of subversive forn snales climed in the god-dam malebox or some enmy of this great cuntry ripped off the male-man or watever. my poisnal view is anyone innerferin with the US post offis shuld git a fare trile and have there hed took off with a chane-saw.

rite me soon as you git this.

your nefew.

13 arpil
dear aunt may
okay. doan say you din git fare warnin. it is the rite of evry amercan to go visit wear he goddam well likes. it is what our four fathers done. if the redskins hadda sent up a smoak single saying hi fellas our hous is your hous any you guys fansy a beer, insted of wear they started wid the arows and the tomahorks and simlar ax of innernatoinal terrism we wouldna had to take self-defense mesures. they culda bin livin in wigscrapers in east harlem by now and gittin bufloburgers on soshul securty along wid the rest of the coon freeloders.

by the time you git this leter you willa bin visited and visited dam good. you wil know you bin visited on account of wear the windows is all bust in and the roof is all ript off and their is smoak comin out your ferncher and the cats insides is all over the yard. you will be reedin this sittin onna pile ruble and wondrin why in hell you din hav the sense to invite me in as an adviser to run your plase and keep it saif from comnism and muslin funmenlism and sardinista dick-hedism and slanty-eyed gookism and i doan know what-all. i gess you bin lissnin to some europ fagot or other or else the lousy innernatoinal marxist conspirsy alredy got to you in wich case tuff tit you ole dingbat you had it comin.

i know their is pinko frigfists out their who wil say i shulda negoshted or i shulda give you time to git out or shulda arst some kine permision from the nieghbers but i say the hell with that our moto is do it to them before they do it to you. eat your hart out perl harber is my view.

i am goin off to stik bootblak on my fase now. their is a hunters moon. i doan know exackly wear you hang out due to wear my teecher is keeping her lip butoned and keeps on teling me you are imagnary but she is just another member

150

of the gutless pasifist femnist wimp conspirsy i say their is nuthin imagnary about the enmies of uncl sam they are all over the hole goddam plase. look under any stoan.

anyway what the hel. i got my airgun i got my slingshot i got my crucifix i got my chane-saw i got my zippo i got my dawg dook. i got more goddam fire-powr than ten thousand ole dames. i culd take out the hole lousy nieghberhood. the way i see it wen it comes to self-defense is you win a few you lose a few.

one things fer sure aunt may. you aint seen nuthin yet.
                                    your nefew.

The Royal Horticultural Society

CRICKLEWOOD FLOWER SHOW

The Old Pesthouse
Cricklewood

May 20-24

MAIN CONCOURSE
THE THRIPS PAVILION

As ever, the Thrips Pavilion is a cynosure for the discerning horticulturalist! Now situated in the Old Greenhouse, which last year's visitors may remember as the New

Greenhouse, the pavilion, thanks to a wonderfully moist 1986 summer, this year boasts a wealth of new exhibits, including Solomon's Leafhopper – rarely seen outside the smarter zoos – a colony of Flea Beetles capable of eating thirty wallflowers an hour, the largest Bean Weevil in the Home Counties, two regiments of Capsid Bugs, and a commune of Sawflies which, while waiting for the roses outside to reach succulence, may be heard keeping their molars in trim by filing their way through what is left of the Old Greenhouse strutwork.

Visitors should be warned that last year's Best Of Show favourites, the Red Spider Mites, are back in force and twice the size: do not, therefore, remain stationary for more than fifteen seconds, since shoes represent a challenge to which this plucky little omnivore is ever on the *qui vive* to rise!

Instead, pass on quickly to the handsome Black Spot display, this year attractively interplanted with Galloping Scab, Powdery Mildew, Spur Blight, and engaging clumps of the hardy perennial, Bacterial Canker. Pause at the door before exiting, and marvel at the fragrant blaze of Rhizome Rot, through which, on the first day at least, odd fragments of iris may still be discerned.

STAND 1
DWARF OAK

Emerging from the Main Concourse, turn left for the justly renowned *bonsai* display of Dwarf Oak, which this year is situated on the New Lawn. Last year, regular visitors will recall, it was situated on the Old Lawn, which is why the Head Gardener took up the Old Lawn and laid the New Lawn.

STAND 2
INTERESTING GOOSEBERRY

Despite this year's severe frost, there appears to be something growing in the renowned Cricklewood Gooseberry

Arbour. On one of the sturdy twigs, there are three little green things, only two of which have legs. From the fact that the two with legs have not attacked the thing without legs, the Head Gardener is of the opinion that this is quite possibly a rare pest-resistant species which could very likely swell into a major berry later in the season.

Alternatively, it is a third thing with legs which is either (a) sleeping, and has folded its legs underneath, or (b) dead, and the legs have shrivelled off. Visitors are respectfully requested not to poke it.

STAND 3
UNORNAMENTAL POND

In the opinion of the Cricklewood judges, far too much attention is paid these days to ornamental ponds. A garden is not, in the salty words of the crusty old Head Gardener, a bloody aquarium, big expensive Oriental fish with sensitive constitutions have no place in an English hortiscape, especially the kind you pay a fortune for at the Hendon Pond Centre and next morning they are belly up and not gold any more, they are covered in sort of cotton wool, you might as well have bought a stone of sprats if you just wanted stuff to float about.

This year, therefore, the Head Gardener is exhibiting his revolutionary Unornamental Pond, which not only saves valuable time by not requiring anyone to stare into it for hours on end on the off-chance that something not yet dead will offer a glimpse of itself shooting between one clump of weed and another, but also does not demand constant maintenance.

Tennis balls from over the fence – once a considerable bone of neighbourly contention during the period when the Head Gardener thought there might have been an expensive live fish still in it somewhere which could have been done a serious mischief by a sudden blow on the head – may safely be left to rot; cats seeking to supplement their diets with takeaway Chinese from the Hendon Pond Centre need not be seen off with half-bricks likely to bounce through the remains of the Old Greenhouse (*Main Concourse*); and drunks believing that they have been invited round of a Sunday morning in order to fill anything ornamental with dog ends, olive stones, corks, matches, Twiglets, and vol-au-vent shards may not only be left to get on with it, but actively encouraged to paddle, so that the surface scum breaks up and the mosquitoes can get out and into the Thrips Pavilion where they belong.

STAND 4
BROWN CORNER

Annual visitors to the Cricklewood Show are in for a real surprise this year! The old Sucker Garden section – hitherto reserved for those plants on which the Head Gardener shelled out a fortune at the Horatio Bottomley Garden Centre on the clear understanding that they would burst into a floribundal explosion calculated to make Vita Sackville-West spin in her mulch, but which in fact went yellow and fell over as soon as the cheque was cleared – has now been refurbished as the Dry Flower Display Centre.

Visitors who believed that such craftwork stopped at teazels, bullrushes, and a few old hydrangea heads stuck in a fake terracotta torso of Alexander the Great will be amazed at what can be done with several truckloads of expensive shrubs! Note especially the mature brown cedar skeleton, sixteen feet high, £80 plus VAT, standing in a mound of its own needles, and what cleverly appears at first sight to be a huge brazil-nut bush but upon closer inspection turns out to be a rhododendron throttled at the root by an interesting goitre the size of a cauliflower.

If there is time, ask to see the mahonia, the osmanthus, and the camellia, a display of everbrowns which the Head Gardener is keeping in a shed as evidence until he works out his closing speech to the jury.

STAND 5
THE SUCKER GARDEN

No relation (*see Stand 4*) to the old Sucker Garden, but a whole new horticultural concept, for which the Head Gardener felt entitled to appropriate the name!

For this is a *true* sucker garden, with a quite breaktaking – and in the opinion of the judges, unparalleled – wealth of such lovely old friends as the Ena Harkness Sucker, the Boule de Neige Sucker, the Arthur Bell Sucker, the Mullard Jubilee Sucker, the Picasso Sucker, and – of course – Her Gracious Majesty The Queen Mother's own special favourite, the Peace Sucker. And this year, for the first time, the Head Gardener is showing the extremely rare Dorothy Perkins Climbing Sucker, which has gone up an acacia tree, according to his notes, 'like a sodding rocket and may very well have Dick bleeding Whittington in it somewhere'.

STAND 6
FUN WITH FENCING

Despite being contained within a mere two hundred perimetric feet, the Cricklewood Show is justly famous for what is probably the greatest variety of fencing in Europe! A six-foot length of Original Featherboarding leads into a sudden unexpected panel of Dark Brown Wattle affixed loosely by a strange steel plate of the Head Gardener's own design to a Very Low Run of Old Planks that in turn join up, by one of an attractively asymmetrical smattering of sporadic Concrete Spurs, to a panel of Light Brown Wattle which, within a very few feet, cunningly avoids blending with a run of Stained Hardboard that, as it moves in the wind, produces a most pleasing groan in the section tacked next to it by Half An Old Arris Rail, this section being Part Original Featherboarding, Part New Featherboarding For Some Reason Two Feet Shorter Than The Other Part, the whole more or less held in place by Antique Gravel Boards attractively bowed to allow dogs' heads from next door to poke through to see if the cat from the other side is still waiting for something to surface in the Unornamental Pond.

The same cunningly insouciant landscaping has gone into the trelliswork that tops certain parts of the fence-run. Visitors will note that there is not only Triangular Trellis and Rectangular Trellis, but also attractive combinations of the two, many tied to one another with up to six different sorts of string and flex, and some lying with unaffected casualness on the ground to facilitate the Head Gardener's novel use of clematis as ground-cover.

STAND 7
GARDEN FURNITURE

New this year is the Big Mouldy Table And Two Peculiarly Warped Benches, developed from last year's Special Teakette Garden Offer Only £29.95. Great fun for the kiddies, who can pick mushrooms off the table and roll Dinkies down the benches, this attractive display is well worth photographing, since it will almost certainly not be around for next year's Show. Something appears to have escaped from the Thrips Pavilion and is rapidly eating its way up the legs.

High on the Hog

BBC Radio York is under siege from animal welfare groups concerned about a programme telling how to cook a hedgehog, which includes the sound of the hedgehog being gutted and stuffed with herbs.

Producer Chris Choi said in the programme's defence: 'We do make it clear that it is not advisable to eat hedgehogs as they can be infested. It is also against the law to deprive a hedgehog of its liberty or to kill it inhumanely. But if you have a suitable hedgehog, there is nothing wrong with cooking it.'

Daily Telegraph

'SPEAKING AS what might reasonably be described as imminent crackling,' said Pigling Bland, 'I cannot but see this as a case of About Bloody Time Too. It is my considered view that the Tiggywinkles of this world ought to have had a lid on 'em well before this, regulo 3, baste frequently, serve on bed of fluffy rice with perhaps a lightly tossed green salad, pour on sauce just before bringing to table, and with it may we suggest a robust bourgeois growth, possibly a Pauillac.'

Across the threadbare Wilton of the Beatrix Potter Day Centre, the glittering nail-head eyes of Mrs Tiggywinkle reddened with venom.

'It's no good glowering at him like that,' said Jemima Puddleduck. 'He has a definite point.'

'The pig is the world's smartest animal,' said Squirrel Nutkin.

'You're after something,' said Pigling Bland.

'That is a trifle harsh,' said Squirrel Nutkin.

'You always were a smarmy little bastard,' said Pigling Bland, unruffled. 'I cannot for the moment spot what is going on in that ratlike head of yours, but it will no doubt come to me in a bit. I am rarely wrong.'

'I was about to say,' snapped Jemima Puddleduck, 'that the point you have got is that in the animal world, we are two nations.'

'Nice one,' nodded Squirrel Nutkin. 'Yours, I imagine, madam?'

'He's off again,' said Pigling Bland. 'How sycophantic can you get?'

'Great word,' murmured Squirrel Nutkin. 'Who would've thought anything had four syllables in it?'

'Two nations,' said Pigling Bland, 'was coined, for your information, by Benjamin Disraeli.' He paused, and throwing out a deft trotter, nudged a small rabbit daydreaming by the fire. 'No relation, I suppose?'

'No,' said Benjamin Bunny.

'Pity,' said Pigling Bland. 'I need a new formal three-piece whistle.'

'I don't follow,' said Benjamin Bunny.

'I thought – had you been a relation – he might have offered me a discount. Possibly chucked in the waistcoat gratis.'

'Personally,' said Peter Rabbit, noticing his small cousin's blushing discomfiture at this, 'I do not like racial jokes.'

'However funny?' enquired Squirrel Nutkin.

'Furthermore,' continued Peter Rabbit, 'I cannot imagine why a pig of all people should wish to direct offensive remarks at Benjamin Disraeli. He never represented a threat to pork, as I understand it.'

'That is exactly my point,' said Pigling Bland. 'It is not easy to extend the hand of friendship to someone who considers you too dirty to roast.'

Mrs Tiggwinkle, sensing that the social wind was suddenly changing in her favour and away from her tormentor's, spoke at last.

'He never ate hedgehog, neither, and I say good luck to him.'

Pigling Bland stared at her for a time.

'What a valuable contribution to the debate!' he said finally. 'I only wish Plato were here with his nib sharpened. However, may I submit, madam, that when it comes to cleanliness, there is something of a difference between a hedgehog and a hog, namely that one of them lives in a hedge. This doubtless explains the hedgehog's hitherto unremarkable absence from top menus: stick *côtelettes d'hérisson provençale* on the table d'hôte, and the Michelin inspectors would be off up the Wimpy before you could unroll their napkin. Your average gourmet does not go looking for places where fleas hop out of the gravy.'

As this, each particular quill upon Mrs Tiggywinkle sprang erect; she might well have hurled herself upon Pigling Bland like some arcane piece of mediaeval ordnance, had he not held up a propitiatory trotter.

'Do not misunderstand me,' he said, quickly. 'There is no shame in being infested, if you are an animal. It goes with the territory. Especially if you are a hedgehog. I should imagine it is extremely difficult evicting the little buggers. Start rooting about in an overcoat like that and you could poke your eye out. All I am saying is that up until now fleas have proved something of a stumbling-block when it came to classic recipes. As far as human beings are concerned, and taking up Mrs Puddleduck's succinct point, there are two distinct categories of animals, those they eat and those they don't, e.g. badgers, moles, water-rats, toads, fieldmice, stoats, weasels, or anything else in the willows.'

'What an interesting critical observation!' cried Squirrel Nutkin. 'What you are saying in your infinite wisdom is that, while they do not eat anything by Kenneth Grahame, they will eat anything by Beatrix Potter.'

'Excluding, up until now, hedgehogs,' nodded Pigling Bland, 'yes. That is why I welcome Mrs Tiggywinkle to the club. It is a big day.'

'They don't eat cats,' observed Tom Kitten, from the mat.

'*Don't eat cats?*' cried Pigling Bland. 'Try walking down Peking High Road sometime! You'd be crispy before you got to the first traffic-light.'

There was a faint plop. Mr Jeremy Fisher had fainted. Pigling Bland looked at him.

'He has probably just remembered the French would pull his legs off,' he observed drily.

'I have often wondered,' said Jemima Puddleduck, 'what they do with the rest of the frog.'

'Hard to say,' replied Pigling Bland. 'They will very likely start gutting it and stuffing it with herbs, if they can pick up Radio York. A nod is a good as a wink over there.'

'*Don't!*' shrieked Mrs Tiggywinkle.

'Pull yourself together,' snapped Jemima Puddleduck. 'You do not seem to realize the opportunity that is being offered the hedgehog world. They have been elevated to delicacy status. When my time comes, I shall be honoured to pass away *à l'orange*, very possibly as a Dish of the Day.'

'Eaten, perhaps, by a senior executive or consultant gynaecologist, exactly,' said Pigling Bland. 'Imagine getting washed down with a '47 Lafite!'

'It is against the law to deprive a hedgehog of its liberty!' cried Mrs Tiggywinkle. 'And what is stuffing us with sage and onion, if not that?'

'Enabling you to realize your full potential,' replied Pigling Bland. 'Showing you there is more to life than mopping up slugs and rolling into balls. I just hope you're suitable, as defined by producer Chris Choi. No gristle or ringworm. Rejection can be a terrible thing. I had a brother who only lived for the day when he could be turned on a spit by a topless wench in a tourist reconstruction of Queen Elizabeth's arrival at Dover. Turned out he had swine fever. Poor sod ended up as a gross of wallets and six pairs of rally gloves.'

'That was never in Beatrix Potter,' said Tom Kitten, 'was it?'

'No,' replied Pigling Bland, 'no, you're right there. She left that one for her son Dennis.'

'You mean . . .'

'Definitely. Can't you tell? It's in the blood. Look at that malicious bastard Mr McGregor, she only called his book *Peter Rabbit* for the uniform edition. Its original title was *The Singing Gardener*.'

They all pondered this silently. It seemed to explain much. It was Squirrel Nutkin who finally spoke.

'People do eat squirrels, don't they, Pigling Bland?' he wheedled.

Pigling Bland looked at him triumphantly.

'I wondered what you were after!' he cried. 'Bloody social climber. Yes, all right, there is a lot of squirrelburger about. Do not give yourself airs, though, sunshine. It is almost entirely take-away. And, of course, only in the North.'

The others looked at him enquiringly.

'Stone me!' cried Pigling Bland. 'Does nobody read the papers? We are not the only ones split into two nations. It is no coincidence that it is Radio *York* doling out hedgehog recipes, it is on direct instructions to the BBC from Norman Tebbit, when he speaks they jump, it has become clear to him that there is no point Northerners getting on their bikes and trying to cross the border, they might as well stay put and live on hedgehog, it is very nutritious with a nice nettle stuffing and . . .'

A tiny cry went up, a tiny chair flew back, and four tiny paws scrabbled for the door, and freedom.

But Mrs Tiggywinkle got no further than the motorway beyond the end of the little front garden. In the few seconds it took the rest to recover and scurry after her, it was all over.

They gathered on the hard shoulder, and stared gloomily at the fast lane.

'Look at that,' said Pigling Bland. 'Pizza.'

The Bespoke Overkill

THE SUNDAY TIMES

5 OCTOBER 1986

No 8,461   Price 50p

Revealed: the secrets of Israel's nuclear arsenal

The hand-lettered fascia board said:

Rappaport & Moss
Bespoke Gents Ware
No Bang Too Large Or Small

I pushed at the door.

It opened. The little bell tinkled.

'Don't slam!' shouted a voice.

I stepped through, and closed the door carefully. The shop smelt of plutonium and herring.

Outside, in the traditional hubbub of Tel Aviv's bustling bomb district, harassed men in armbands pushed clanging racks of missiles along the narrow pavements, haggard sales reps dragged their samples in and out of a hundred overstocked shopfronts, frantic knots of thermonuclear wholesalers scuttled, yelling, among the hurtling delivery vans and their cursing drivers, outraged designers stamped their feet at sweating patent agents, warehouse foremen clouted factory runners, errand boys with trays of lemon tea collided with office juniors struggling under piles of order books and invoices – but, in here, all was suddenly and strangely quiet.

Except for a faint far pattering beneath my feet, as of carpet slippers over dry flagstones. After a moment or two, a pink and hairless head emerged from a trapdoored gap in the middle of the floor, and peered around, until its half-moon spectacles settled on me.

'Stocktaking,' he explained. 'Give a slam, anything could happen. I wouldn't like to be responsible. We got some slightly soiled Sidewinders down there you only have to look at twice.'

'I quite understand,' I said.

'Ask me why we bought them in the first place.'

'Why did you buy them in the first place?'

'Don't ask.'

He climbed out, puffing, and patted the white dust off, gently.

'Rappaport,' he said. He pushed the spectacles on to his forehead. 'What can I do for you?'

'I'd like a bomb,' I said.

He pulled the spectacles down again, and looked at me over the wire rims.

'If you wanted a pound walnuts,' he said, 'you'd be next door.' He removed the spectacles, and his waistcoat being undone, polished them slowly with the end of his tie.

'This bomb. It's for you, or a gift?'

'For me.'

He took a small black notebook from his waistcoat pocket, and clicked his ballpoint.

'What kind of price range are we talking here?'

'I'm not really sure,' I said. 'I'll, er, I'll know it when I see it.'

Mr Rappaport shrugged.

'Listen, whatever you say. Pressure we can all do without.' He pointed to a sign, which read *Please Look Around And Waste Our Valuable Time Without Obligation*. 'I just don't want you should be embarrassed. You see something in a nice

164

cobalt, say, it suits you down to the ground – you should pardon the expression – and you say perfect, how much, and I tell you, and it's outside your price range, how will we both feel? Terrible is how we'll both feel.'

'I understand,' I said.

'I'll call Moss,' he said.

'Moss!' he called, into the hole.

'I'm coming,' cried Moss. 'I only got two pair of hands.'

'That Moss,' said Rappaport, 'what a comedian. Always a wisecrack.' He laid a hand on my arm. 'From mutations, you don't have to worry. Everything comes straight from the factory, two wrappings, official seals. Don't talk to me about spotless, you can eat off the floor down there.'

A second head appeared in the trapdoor, a thinner head, wispy-haired, hollow-eyed, lugubrious of mien.

'Meet Mr Moss,' said Mr Rappaport. 'A diamond.'

'From the wages,' murmured Mr Moss, 'a rhinestone.'

'This gentleman,' said Mr Rappaport, 'is looking for a bomb.'

Mr Moss climbed out, sighing, and rearranged his thin limbs.

'Nuclear?' he enquired.

'Naturally, nuclear!' snapped Mr Rappaport. 'What are we all of a sudden, a flea market?'

His assistant looked at him for a time. He blew his nose.

'Conventional is also nice,' he said, finally. 'For conventional, what were we? A byword was what we were.'

'Conventional was good to us,' conceded Mr Rappaport. 'When did I say different? Times change, Sam.'

'Change, change,' muttered Mr Moss. 'Conventional is always in fashion. A gentleman should always own a couple items conventional. Discreet, not loud.' He turned to me. 'It's for a formal occasion?'

'I'm sorry?' I said.

'A big affair. An invasion, a war, something you'd like to declare?'

'Possibly,' I said. 'I'm not exactly certain.'

Moss looked at Rappaport.

'Young people these days', he said. 'What do they know?'

'He's not wrong,' said Rappaport to me. 'Once upon a time, formal was formal, casual was casual, you knew where you were. Customers were selective. The occasion called for ten tons high explosive, ten tons high explosive is what it got, you needed a small piece napalm, you ordered a small piece napalm.'

'Today,' said Moss, 'who knows from precision bombing? Personally, I blame Vietnam. Fifty thousand tons HE from ten miles up for a *bridge*? I used to watch it on the television, it broke my heart. Wonderful materiel, and what did they do with it?'

'Cowboys,' said Rappaport. 'Never mind the quality, feel the width.'

'It's simply,' I said, 'that I'm not quite sure what the requirement will be. Is there anything sort of, well, all-purpose?'

Moss sighed.

'We're talking bespoke,' he enquired, 'or ready-to-drop?'

'Under the circumstances,' I said, 'I suppose something off the peg would be better. I could see what I was getting.'

'You want a bomb, a missile, a satellite, what?' enquired Mr Moss, somewhat irritably. 'What kind of delivery system are we talking here?'

'A straightforward bomb,' I said, 'I think.'

'Straightforward,' echoed Mr Rappaport. He barked a short, dry laugh. 'You hear, Sam?'

'If it was straightforward,' said Mr Moss, 'where would we be?'

'The Bahamas is where we'd be,' replied Mr Rappaport. 'Antibes, possibly.'

'Florida is bad?'

Mr Rappaport reached behind the littered counter, took down a sample book, licked his thumb, turned the pages. Moss peered over his shoulder. Rappaport paused. Moss nodded.

'If you want a plain vehicle-delivered bomb,' he said, swivelling the book around towards me, 'you couldn't do better than this one. A very popular number. Always in fashion.'

'It looks a little big,' I said.

'Big is the thing these days,' said Moss. 'Ask anyone. A generous cut is the style. Read the magazines, you'll see.'

'Even so . . .'

'Do they do it in a five-kiloton?' asked Rappaport.

'No,' said Moss. 'We'd have to alter.' He drew a piece of chalk from his waistcoat pocket. 'Take it in a bit here, make a little dart there, you wouldn't even notice the seam.'

'Could be very smart,' nodded Rappaport, 'in a five-kiloton. While we're at it, you know what I'd do? I'd make up the case in a nice light-weight. Pass me the swatch.'

Mr Moss reached beneath the counter, and handed up a bundle of metal plates on a ring.

'Ruthenium is nice,' he said to me. 'Feel.'

'It's not too thin?' I said.

'What do you want,' cried Moss, 'shrapnel? This is a nuclear device. If you want a hand grenade, go to Feldman!'

'Look,' said Rappaport, soothingly, 'how about we do the case in ruthenium and set the fins off in a nice twelve-ounce blue tungsten?'

'You're giving him a bespoke bomb at ready-to-drop prices?' enquired Moss.

'It's not all about money, Sam,' said Rappaport. 'A craftsman is a craftsman. The gentleman walked in the shop, right away I said: *that's a five-kiloton in a nice ruthenium-tungsten man-made.* So we do it at cost, so what? We have a satisfied customer. If he likes it in nuclear, who knows, next season maybe he'll come back and we'll make it up in biological.'

'There I'd argue,' said Moss. 'This is basically a traditional dirty bomb. Full in the waste. Sure, it's a little old-fashioned, it's been around a few years, but it's classical. With a bomb like this, you could walk in anywhere.'

'You don't see it in a nice contemporary neutron?'

'It would take all the life out of it,' said Moss.

Mr Rappaport shut the book, and looked up.

'Should be ready Thursday,' he said. 'I can't promise, I got two cutters off sick, you know how it is. But we'll do our best.'

'Well,' I said, 'could I let you know, it was more in the nature of a general enqu . . .'

'Listen,' said Mr Rappaport, 'you don't want to commit yourself, so don't commit yourself. Take it home, see how you like it, if it doesn't deter anybody for seven days, bring it back, we'll refund. After all, we can always shift it, am I right, Sam?'

Mr Moss, rolling up his tape-measure, nodded.

'How much can it hurt?' he said.